Knowledge Networks for Business Growth

T0238566

Andrea Back · Ellen Enkel
Georg von Krogh
(Editors)

Knowledge Networks
for Business Growth

With 28 Figures

 Springer

Professor Dr. Andrea Back
IWI-HSG – Institute of Information Management
University of St. Gallen
Müller-Friedberg-Strasse 8
9000 St. Gallen
Switzerland
andrea.back@unisg.ch

Dr. Ellen Enkel
ITEM-HSG – Institute of Technology Management
University of St. Gallen
Dufourstrasse 40 a
9000 St. Gallen
Switzerland
ellen.enkel@unisg.ch

Georg von Krogh
Professor of Strategic Management and Innovation
ETH Zurich
Department of Management, Technology, and Economics
KPL H14, Kreuzplatz 5
8032 Zurich
Switzerland
gvkrogh@ethz.ch

ISBN 978-3-642-06960-4   e-ISBN 978-3-540-33073-8

Cataloging-in-Publication Data

Springer is a part of Springer Science+Business Media

springeronline.com

© Springer Berlin · Heidelberg 2010

Hardcover-Design: Erich Kirchner, Heidelberg

Preface

Companies are constantly searching for new ways of creating higher profit and a larger market share. Growth seems to be the most appropriate tactic for surviving economical difficult times. Investigating new instruments and methods with which to support a company's growth strategy thus seems key in gaining a competitive advantage. It is strongly believed that knowledge management is one of the answers to this challenge. It can support strategic goals such as the improvement of efficiency, the minimization of risk and an increase in innovation, but knowledge management also has inherent potentials that have not as yet been leveraged. Knowledge networks are an extension of knowledge management in that they connect knowledge owners throughout the company. This book takes a closer look at the potential of knowledge networks to support a company's growth strategy.

Knowledge networks are an organizational form with which to support knowledge sharing and creation within a company. They are comprised of a group of key experts who are the custodians of a well-defined knowledge domain that is important for the achievement of company strategy and the attainment of business benefits. Linking knowledge networks to companies' growth strategy enables organizations to support this strategy actively and gain competitive advantage. This book focuses on this link between networks and growth strategy: the concept of knowledge networks for growth.

There are many areas that support companies' growth strategy. Theory shows that supporting internal innovation and integrating external knowledge sources are successful strategies for profitable growth. Within these two strategies, three areas were focused on to test the concept of knowledge networks for growth: customer knowledge integration, support of internal innovation initiatives and integration after mergers and acquisition. Following an action research approach and based on the results of prior research on knowledge networks, we created a framework for knowledge networks for growth and adapted it for the three focus areas. This framework is derived from theory and projects undertaken with three major companies in the field of knowledge management: Hewlett Packard, RWE and Unilever.

The three partner companies have experience with knowledge management and knowledge networking and explore the value of networks crossing the boundaries of "normal" organizational forms to support knowledge sharing and creation. They have an explicit growth strategy and are constantly searching for instruments to improve their performance.

In February 2000, the research project "knowledge networks for growth" started at the University of St. Gallen (Switzerland)[1] and aimed, over a two-year period, to develop and test the concept of knowledge networks to support the mentioned growth strategies. Two knowledge managers from each company and five researchers from the University formed the core team of the bilateral research project to test and implement the adapted framework. They also held regular workshops to support knowledge sharing between these companies and the researchers.

As a major result of this research, general factors were deduced that could be implemented in all networks by adapting the framework for individual companies. We argue that by adjusting these factors it is also possible to adapt the knowledge network framework for other growth areas like brand- and marketing-oriented networks or strategic networks. Building knowledge networks for growth means adapting the framework for the specific growth area as well as to the company's specifics.

In line with our approach, the first article of the book discusses the concept of knowledge networks for growth and makes general recommendations. Three cases present the bilateral projects and show the adaptation and implementation of the framework for knowledge networks for growth in the focus areas of customer knowledge integration at Hewlett Packard, the integration after a merger within RWE and an innovation network approach at Unilever. Each case ends with learnings for other companies and recommendations for a general framework in the mentioned fields.

But this book not only aims to illustrate the management of the concept of knowledge networks for growth in practice, but also gives knowledge managers and network leaders hands-on guidelines to set up and adapt these knowledge networks. The cases are therefore followed by a methodology for setting up knowledge networks for growth with examples given and steps to follow. The appendix includes templates to gather data with which to support this adaptation.

---

[1] The research project "knowledge networks for growth" was part of the activities of the research centre KnowledgeSource of the University of St. Gallen. KnowledgeSource is formed by the collaboration of Prof. Georg von Krogh (Director of the Institute of Management) and Prof. Andrea Back (Director of the Institute of Information Management) and is led by Ellen Enkel as project manager.

In economically hard times, the call to prove value in respect of costs becomes louder. Management would like to see a relationship between cost and value and return on investment (ROI). It is crucial to prove performance and value in order to get the attention and the support which activities, especially knowledge management activities, need. The methodology part is therefore followed by an article presenting a new approach to measure knowledge networks for growth, called "the integrated measurement system". This system combines external and internal methods with which to measure and monitor the performance of knowledge networks as well as their value for companies' growth strategy.

A book like this requires close cooperation from all the companies that participated in our research. We learned much from the managers with whom we worked. In a candid and professional way they shared their knowledge and experience, and helped to create and test our proposed concept by being open in discussions and generous with their time. Beside our partners in the core team, the people who were excited by our ideas and supportive of our efforts also played a role in supporting us. There are too many to name, but we owe special thanks to our core research team members Claudia Ulrich and Ewald Kollakowski of the Hewlett Packard support center in Ratingen (Germany), Kordula Schulte and Carl-Heinrich Kruse from RWE Net as well as Anita Pos and Manfred Aben from the Knowledge Management Group of Unilever N.V.

There are also numerous employees and managers within these companies who supported our efforts in the bilateral projects, opened doors for us and gave us feedback on our work. We owe special thanks to Thomas Kayser of Unilever, a core team member in the first year, who often pointed out major factors and helped us to develop the framework further through his valuable feedback. We also thank Heinrich Christen and Markus Aeschimann from Gemini Ernst & Young for their support in this research project's first year.

Our academic debts are large as well. Robert Galliers and Dorothy Leonard have been a great influence on our thinking about knowledge sharing and supporting innovation. The core team who contributed directly to this book was unbelievably committed and professional. In St. Gallen, Grzegorz Gurgul and Maria Rumyantseva, two doctoral students and research associates, played an important role in researching and writing parts of this book.

Valuable contributions to our research also came from the doctoral students Michael Gibbert, Stefanos Vassiliadis and Alexei Makarevitch, who worked on this project part time. It was wonderful to have a helpful and enthusiastic editor in Ilse Evertse, who believed in our idea and provided invaluable and highly professional editorial assistance. She kept us on track while encouraging us to explore the complexity of the topic by keeping it reader friendly and highly interesting. Her valuable comments and advice in the final stage of the book helped a great deal.

St. Gallen, June 2006

Ellen Enkel

Andrea Back

Georg von Krogh

Table of Content

1 The Concept of Knowledge Networks for Growth

Ellen Enkel[1], Andrea Back[2] and Georg von Krogh[2]

[1]Project Manager Research Center KnowledgeSource, University of St. Gallen, Switzerland

[2]Head Research Center KnowledgeSource, University of St. Gallen, Switzerland

Abstract

This article illustrates our concept of knowledge networks for growth, i.e. social networks that support companies' growth strategy by their ability to share and create knowledge. We adapted the framework of intra-organizational networks to set up networks in three different growth areas: growth through the acquisition of external knowledge and its integration through merger and acquisitions; the support of internal innovation processes through the coordination of the innovation activities of independent business groups or units, and, lastly, growth through the integration of customers' tacit knowledge in the internal innovation process.

The article first discusses which growth fields can be supported by special knowledge management activities and which prerequisites they require. Thereafter the reasons for knowledge networks being the correct choice with which to support companies' growth strategy are elaborated on. Simultaneously, the organizational forms of communities of practice, communities of interest, project teams and formal knowledge networks are compared according to certain characteristics.

The next section describes how knowledge networks for growth function in practice. Three examples, derived from our research, illustrate the respective cases of a customer integration network, a post-merger integration network and an innovation coordination network. The examples are discussed according to the general components of knowledge networks and point out certain obstacles linked to the specific growth fields investigated. The section concludes by pointing out important components and their adaptation that might make the difference between success and failure.

Introduction

In a "knowledge society" in which individual and organizational knowledge can make a difference in gaining a competitive advantage, the management of knowledge is crucially important for all companies. When taking the challenges of modern times, like shorter product cycles, globalization and the mobility of employees, into account, companies' reaction is generally to cut costs and restructure their organization. Besides achieving a reduction of costs and product reorientation, both these results also lead to the isolation of single business units and the termination of knowledge flows between former colleagues. The resultant company structures are highly cost efficient, but lack the ability to learn from the failures and successes across the company, or to use their synergies professionally. These deficiencies, in turn, lead to independent knowledge islands that lack effective knowledge transfer and creation mechanisms with which to gain the abilities needed to compete successfully. Effective knowledge management guarantees that companies will be able to leverage their knowledge pool in order to create innovation – the only sustainable competitive advantage when cost cutting has reduced costs to a minimum.

The literature on how to achieve effective knowledge management is vast, but provides very few managerial guidelines on how to set up and use the instruments efficiently. In recent years, organizational forms such as communities of practice and knowledge networks have gained increasing attention. Their logic is to complement a company's matrix structure in order to support the transfer and creation of knowledge between independent business units, across functions, hierarchies or geographical distances. Bringing together the right people within a company to share knowledge and create the new knowledge that might result in innovation seems to be the obvious answer to problems arising from knowledge islands and obviates the need for a major restructuring. But setting up successful communities of practice or knowledge networks is even more difficult than setting up successful project teams. In a project team, each individual "only" needs to fulfill his task as determined by his expertise, while members of communities and networks have to share their personal knowledge to gain advantage for their company in which knowledge is regarded as one of the last differentiating factors when competing on an individual level. It becomes even more difficult if the company tries to manage these groups in order to direct them towards fields in which the company requires the sharing of existing knowledge or the creation of new knowledge.

To find answers to the problems briefly described above, our research during the past years focused on how to create successful knowledge networks and how to focus them on fields that support companies' growth strategy. This article describes the findings gained and presents a blueprint for knowledge networks that support companies' growth strategies. To do so, we first identify growth fields where effective knowledge management through organizational forms could add value. We then develop the concept of knowledge networking by differentiating between networks and other organizational forms for knowledge sharing, such as communities and project teams, which then leads to the framework for knowledge networks for growth.

Knowledge Networking as a Strategy for Company Growth

This section will discuss which growth fields in companies' strategy require a certain form of governance to leverage their value. The form of governance seems to play a crucial role in growth strategies that facilitate the capability of integrating new knowledge, e.g., after an M&A as well as when creating internal innovation. The support of a company's growth strategy has certain requirements regarding knowledge sharing and creation. This section therefore also discusses knowledge-based organizational forms as possible governance structures with a view to identifying their potential. After comparing specific organizational forms, the concept of intra-organizational knowledge networks is examined.

Leveraging Companies' Internal and External Growth Potentials

By using Fortune 1000 companies in the period 1988 to 1993 as a sample, Mercer Consulting (Gertz and Baptista, 1995) classified the American business world into four groups that they pithily named: Shrinkers, Cost Cutters, Unprofitable Growers, and Profitable Growers. An analysis of profitable growth companies leads to two important ways in which these companies can be understood: first by the strategy they follow, and, second, by what they do to make these strategies successful. Admittedly, every business strategy is unique. However, there are some broad groupings of key issues that offer an explanation for profitable growth: *customer centricity and new products and services*. Recent studies support this result (see e.g. Moser and Moukanas, 2002, p. 13). Kim and Mauborgne (Kim and Mauborgne, 1997) offer a corresponding argument when they recognize the opportunities revealed by what Drucker (2002) describes as a purposeful reconnaissance of the environment. Companies achieve sustained high growth by pursuing value innovation – shaping conditions in an industry and pursuing value for customers in quantum leaps.

The result from the Mercer study doesn't surprise theorists or managers who know that innovations, which lead to new products and services and customer-centric behavior, are needed to achieve profitable growth. But since innovation is seen as the driving force of the 21st century, we need to search for strategies and instruments to support internal growth through innovation. Knowledge management, and especially knowledge sharing and creation are viewed as fruitful ways of influencing companies' internal growth capabilities (von Krogh and Venzin, 1995). Knowledge is regarded as one important source of innovation, therefore a knowledge-based view of the company can throw light on how to attain sustained, profitable growth through value innovation.

Improving companies' internal knowledge sharing and creation can lead to innovation and, in turn, to company growth. This can be combined with a customer-centric strategy: if a company is able to integrate customer knowledge to gain innovation, this should lead to new customer-oriented products and services. During those times when the product life cycle is reduced, product development time increases steadily and competitors too aren't slumbering, it is very important to launch customer-oriented products and services. This saves important resources, guarantees competitiveness and increases customer loyalty. It seems mandatory for a company to integrate its customers and to create customer-oriented products and services. The reason is obvious: some customers have a very profound and useful real life experience with, and therefore valuable knowledge of, a company's products. Their experience and knowledge may lead to product and service improvements, but only if an enterprise listens to and taps the customer experience and knowledge. Only the establishment and the consequent realization of customer-oriented strategies as a strong driver can lead to a better competitive advantage.

This, finally, leads to the point where you can actually facilitate innovation through the right environment. With this in mind, it is necessary to stress the importance of the appropriate form of governance with which to create new knowledge. The example of the World Bank, as used by Wood and Hamel (Wood and Hamel, 2002), shows how a network structure could facilitate internal innovation immensely and what is required to follow the networking strategy successfully.

One other important strategy for company growth needs to be mentioned as well: external growth through mergers and acquisitions. This strategy follows the assumption that buying knowledge that you don't have in your company will lead to innovations and, therefore, company growth. The main objectives of merger and acquisitions are rather similar, e.g., the increase of shareholder value, a response to revolutionary change in the industry, gaining an asset in the form of funds and the exploitation of the economy of scale and scope. Since shorter product cycles increase competition and make organic growth seem excessively time-consuming in many industries, numerous managers consider acquisition to be an attractive means of swiftly expanding a firm's knowledge base. "In today's economy, building work teams from scratch can be yesterday's luxury. So, when you can't build fast enough, you buy." (Wysocki, 1997). However, acquiring firms have discovered that the sharing and utilization of knowledge through acquisitions can be a difficult task. It is contingent on the successful integration of the acquired unit, and very often the process of integrating fails outright. Since 1997, corporations world-wide have spent $5 trillion on mergers and acquisitions. In 2000 alone, more than 9,000 M&A deals took place. With so much shareholder value riding on these actions, one would expect the process to have been standardized. Yet in 83% of 700 large mergers, the stock price of the combined organization did not rise above those of the single entities (Mergerstat, 2000).

As far as employees are concerned, the most significant problems and obstacles during the integration of two companies are not the technical systems or organizational layouts that can be solved reasonably easily. Changing employees' mindset and the integration of the two knowledge bases are the actual difficult tasks. This is especially true if knowledge management initiatives have been neglected during the post-merger integration – after this period obstructions to the free dissemination of knowledge within the company become more difficult to overcome. A merger or an acquisition entails a reorganization of the company, which should be accomplished during the integration of the two companies. During the reorganization, the employees' social networks are destroyed. Ways of knowledge sharing and exchanging experiences are usually terminated due to the creation of new business units, through layoffs or through forced early retirement. Post-merger integration measures tend to be too brief to ensure the sharing of tacit knowledge, nor do they focus on this.

Critical factors for customer decisions, experience of new methods of implementation, and work approaches are examples of knowledge that often remains undocumented. Besides the mentioned barriers, there are further knowledge risks that could be factors in the failure of knowledge integration during mergers and acquisitions. These comprise uncertainty regarding the acquired knowledge assets, employee mistrust of the merger or acquisition, problems of scope caused by employees having similar abilities, and power conflicts among employees. Employees are appointed to new business units, and are often cut off from their established social ties within the company. When the situation is exacerbated by the two sets of employees being mutually prejudiced against each other, these employees remain in their detruncated social networks, resulting in poor knowledge sharing.

Although knowledge management literature has mentioned the potential of acquisitions as a means of gaining access to new knowledge, and acquisition literature has stressed the importance of knowledge sharing after acquisitions in order to create value, few studies have explicitly focused on the sharing of knowledge in mergers or acquisitions – particularly on the factors facilitating such a sharing and the tools required to ensure its efficiency. Research proves that there is a correlation between the mode of governance and knowledge integration intensity (Leonard-Barton, 1995). Only when these correlate, is the M&A likely to have the highest potential for knowledge integration and the creation of new technological capabilities. It was found that the difficulty and the challenge of the integration process are not the result of the sharing of strategic capabilities, the challenge is in fact to create the appropriate atmosphere that will support capability sharing (Haspelagh and Jemison, 1991).

To summarize the arguments incorporated in the section above: there are two ways to create sustained profitable growth, the first is through cost cutting and the second is by acquiring new market segments through value innovation. It was pointed out that only new products and services as well as customer centricity will lead to value innovation and therefore to sustained, profitable growth. Knowledge is a major source of innovation, consequently we follow a knowledge perspective by identifying an important precondition for innovation: knowledge creation. Two ways were described to create new knowledge for value innovation: by improving internal knowledge sharing, or by acquiring new knowledge through mergers and acquisitions (M&A).

If companies decide to acquire access to new knowledge for company growth via M&A (an external growth strategy), knowledge integration and sharing are crucial to create the proposed synergies and innovations. The appropriate instrument should be able to create the right atmosphere for knowledge sharing as well as being able to support the integration of knowledge through the mode of governance, which creates a facilitating environment. Knowledge management as well as M&A literature still fails to mention appropriate managerial instruments with which to facilitate these processes. However, such instruments would need to be adapted to meet the requirements for knowledge integration and creation as identified in the above section. This adaptation will lead to an instrument with which to follow an internal growth strategy through innovation and, by integrating external and internal sources of knowledge efficiently, it will facilitate an external growth strategy and provide the appropriate environment for knowledge creation. Such an instrument can, if located in areas directly related to company growth, support the strategy of profitable growth.

In the following section, the question is raised regarding which organizational form best supports knowledge sharing and creation with which to pursue growth strategies. Consequently, different organizational forms are compared according to their potential to fulfill this aim.

Forms of Governance for Knowledge Sharing and Integration

Knowledge management literature of the past few years has stressed knowledge-based organizational forms that support the matrix organization's knowledge management (Davenport and Prusak, 1998; Back et al., 2005; Wenger et al., 2002). In picturing the organization as a complex structure of different layers, with the hierarchical structure forming only one of these layers, it becomes apparent that knowledge flows between the different layers need to be supported by knowledge management. Fig. 1.1 illustrates some of the ties that create a multinational company from an R&D perspective.

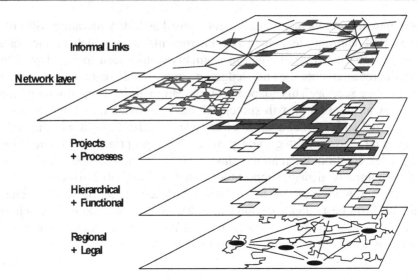

Fig. 1.1 Ties that build an organization (Source: Gassmann and Enkel, 2005)

From a knowledge management perspective, knowledge transfer and creation within the company is mandatory and its organizational structure should support this. Those obstacles that a multinational company needs to overcome are illustrated in the following example. Multinational companies have research and development centers in different regions of the world in order to access innovation clusters' knowledge and contacts, or to benefit from low labor costs or favorable tax laws. Transferring knowledge between the different sites is itself regarded as a major challenge.

Besides this regionally dispersed structure, the hierarchical structure of the company links the different (mainly independent) business units or product groups in order to enable knowledge flows between the established links. The independent nature of some business units or product groups might stimulate them to act as competitors instead of partners under the same company umbrella. If knowledge is regarded as a success factor with which to gain budgets or create revenue, this negatively influences the free transfer of knowledge.

Business units, departments or product groups cooperate through processes along the value chain or additional projects. Similar to competition on a business group level forming a major obstacle to the transfer of knowledge on the hierarchical layer, additional individual competition on the project or process level too forms a barrier. Not all employees are, furthermore, connected through processes or projects.

Additional links between individuals provide informal networks and work relationships within a company as well as with individuals outside the company. Those informal relationships, e.g., with employees in the same field of a profession, or with the same private interests, help individuals to exchange and gain additional knowledge that the established formal structure can't provide. But informal links are limited and mainly serve the employee to gain personal advantage. During the last few years companies have recognized the value of these informal links and actively seek ways to formalize these relationships in order to manage them to create corporate value as well. Connecting the right employees in order to share knowledge and create new knowledge for the company is a benefit that companies want to gain. Communities of practice and knowledge networks comprise two approaches to formalizing those links and subsequently, build and new additional organizational layer. The following section will elaborate on the differences between various approaches in respect of their structure, management and attainable values.

The concept of knowledge networking can be regarded as on a par with communities of practice, project teams or task forces, to name only a few organizational forms. The following section will shortly discuss the potentials of these organizational forms with the focus on the support of company growth and will argue for a knowledge-networking approach. Based on the potentials of knowledge networks for knowledge sharing and integration, a concept of knowledge networks for growth is developed.

Besides knowledge networks, other organizational forms are used to support the line organization through the sharing of knowledge and the facilitating of the creation of new knowledge, e.g., communities of practice, project teams or task forces. Although they can be differentiated from knowledge networks with regards to structure and purpose, the boundaries are blurred. In general, knowledge networks combine the positive knowledge-sharing capabilities of a community of practice with the manageable task solving, or orientation, of a project team focusing on business processes. Table 1.1 provides an overview of the main differences.

Table 1.1 Differences between the organizational forms (Source: Enkel, 2005)

	Community of Interest	Community of Practice	Task Force/ Project Team	Knowledge Network
Characteristics				
Description	Persons connected through their common interest	Persons connected through their common practice	Time-restricted cooperation between practitioners to reach a specific project goal	Connection between experts across the company to exchange knowledge to reach a specific goal
Aims and working mode	Voluntary and self-directed knowledge exchange	Voluntary and self-directed knowledge exchange	Selected members focus their individual skills on the project work	Identified experts focus on knowledge exchange in their area of expertise
Management	Self-directed	Self-directed	Management through working plan	Balance between self-direction and management
Degree of formalization	Informal structure	Informal structure	Formalized structure	Formalized structure
Setting up	Emergent	Emergent	Deliberate	Deliberate
Members' Knowledge	Similar experience of a different quality	Similar experience and homogeneous knowledge	Homogenous and/or complementary knowledge and skills	Homogenous knowledge of high quality
Motivation	Motivated through personal interest	Motivated through personal interest	Motivated through recognition and task	Motivated through recognition and task
Lifetime	Perpetual	Perpetual	Project related	Perpetual
Resources/ Costs	Low cost personnel and infrastructure	Low cost personnel and infrastructure	Middle to high cost personnel, infrastructure and management	Middle to high cost personnel, infrastructure and management

The above table describes the differences between the organizational forms of communities of interest, communities of practice, project teams and knowledge networks. Knowledge networks combine elements of all the structures. Networks, like project teams, can have a formalized structure and working mode, be focused on tasks and be reasonably to highly costly to maintain. Then again, similar to communities, they can also be focused on high quality knowledge sharing and creation. Knowledge networks are as perpetual as communities but, like project teams, are emergently built. The management of knowledge networks is a balance between self-direction and freedom and therefore lies between the community and project approaches. The described attributes of knowledge networks seem to make them ideal for sharing and creating new knowledge, but only a closer look at the concept of knowledge networking can clarify this issue.

Clarifying the Concept of Intra-organizational Knowledge Networking

The underlying assumptions behind knowledge networks as an instrument for knowledge sharing are that valuable tacit knowledge – which is needed to create new knowledge and the resultant innovations – can only be shared through human interaction over an extended period of time (von Krogh et al., 2001a). Managing tacit knowledge requires the creation of an organizational form that connects knowledge agents with the valuable tacit knowledge that should be shared and surrounding them with the appropriate environment needed. The concept of intra-organizational knowledge networks is focused on knowledge sharing rather than knowledge creation and the integration of external sources (Enkel, 2005; Seufert et al., 1999). The concept of knowledge networks for growth is based on these initial ideas and has been developed to include company growth.

Knowledge networks focus on the members' knowledge exchange. They are social networks that can be defined as "a specific set of linkages among a defined set of actors, with the additional property that the characteristics of these as a whole may be used to interpret the social behavior of the actors involved" (Alba, 1982, p. 40; Lincoln, 1982; Mitchell, 1969, p. 2; Tichy et al., 1979, p. 507). The term network focuses on the social relationship between the members. "Most important, in an age of rapidly proliferating knowledge, the central domain is a social network that absorbs, creates, transforms, buys, sells, and communicates knowledge. Its stronghold is the knowledge embedded in a dense web of social, economic, contractual, and administrative relationships" (Badaracco, 1991, pp. 13-14), this means that a network can be regarded as the ideal form for storing and sharing knowledge.

The term knowledge network is therefore used to signify a number of people, their resources and the relationships between them, who are assembled in order to accumulate and use knowledge – primarily by means of knowledge creation and sharing processes – for the purpose of creating value for the company. In more detail, this means that a knowledge network is a recognized and explicitly empowered group of key experts of a well-defined knowledge domain, which is key to the achievement of company strategy and the attainment of business benefits. Knowledge networks can be regarded as instruments for knowledge management, since the network structure includes the ability to connect those knowledge agents (knowledge owners, and experts) within a company who – due to the hierarchical and functional barriers of the line organization – are not connected. In short, networks as communities provide a platform for knowledge sharing between their members. On this network level, knowledge management is mainly a knowledge owner management, meaning the network should support its members and the knowledge process by providing an appropriate environment and tools.

Based on action research projects with companies (see Back et al., 2005 and 2006), we developed the following reference model of knowledge networks (Fig. 1.2). A knowledge network is influenced by three layers, which also form its structure. Network action occurs in the environment of a company. Network members' action is influenced by the management system of which they are part, the corporate culture in which they live and act, and the organizational structure, such as the type of hierarchy or the regional distance (in the figure below, the layer of the facilitating conditions). All these aspects influence their behavior within the network, e.g., if there are flat hierarchies and a knowledge-friendly culture that support knowledge sharing between all employees, network members act differently than they would if they were part of a very hierarchical structure and bureaucratic culture in which individual knowledge is seen as having a competitive advantage. At the start of the network, the members' cooperation with the surrounding environment plays a crucial role and can be a barrier to overcome, or a supportive factor. Later, when people trust one another and share their first successful working experiences, the network creates its own environment that can be different from the corporate environment. But until such time one needs to isolate counterproductive factors and strengthen supportive ones to set up a successful knowledge network.

It is not only the environment that influences network action, the processes within the network and their link to the company's business processes, play a crucial role as well. To create value for the company by fulfilling certain tasks in order to reach the proposed goals, the members need to act in defined processes. These processes should enable the transfer and creation of knowledge, which is the main reason for the network's existence, but should focus on the business fields or processes that the company wants to support.

Likewise, the selection of network members, who need to follow the process line, is crucial for the network's success or failure. Only the right people with the right knowledge, and with the motivation and ability to share it, can build a successful knowledge network. E.g., if the company wants to coordinate its innovation activities better in order to reduce redundancies and create synergies between independent business, or product groups, the company can support knowledge sharing between the business groups by setting up a knowledge network with the portfolio managers of the individual groups. The company needs to select people as network members who recognize the value of sharing their knowledge and have the right knowledge of innovation projects and strategies in their business group.

To motivate people to share their knowledge, to acknowledge their need to gain individual value, to motivate the business group management to free their best people from part of their daily work in order to meet in the network, the network needs to achieve value for the business group as well. Last but not least, the company that sets up and supports the network action needs to gain corporate value. As far as values are concerned, an appropriate performance measurement needs to be integrated to monitor the network action and help identify areas of improvement. Over and above the knowledge processes that occur, the network can only reveal its full value if its actions are closely linked to the company's business processes. To return to our example above, the network of portfolio managers should not only exchange undefined knowledge, but should share knowledge about their innovation activities in order to cooperate in future innovation projects and share learnings and best practices about these activities within their business group. The network action is closely linked with the company's processes when the outcomes of the network are integrated and acted upon. This should result in cost reduction and an increasing rate of successfully launched innovation projects.

To support the (knowledge and business) processes and help to create an appropriate environment, the most effective tools should be integrated. The third layer of the network's architecture describes the topology of the network as well as the tools necessary to support the network or overcome barriers (Back et al., 2005). Information and communication tools play a crucial role, e.g., by enabling the network members to communicate outside meetings, by providing the facilities for a successful meeting, or by helping to capture and store explicit knowledge that is necessary for the network's action. Remaining within the example above, the network of portfolio managers needs to have a proper meeting venue for their monthly meeting, needs to have access to their new electronic innovation process management system in order to create transparency about the status of existing projects etc. Some environmental factors, like meeting frequency and pleasant surroundings, can be influenced directly. Other environmental factors, such as the corporate structure and culture, can only be influenced indirectly by establishing a fruitful relationship across hierarchical barriers or openly sharing knowledge. The latter might lead to the loss of an individual competitive advantage in the short run, but could lead to a better working relationship and knowledge of best practices and valuable learnings in the long run.

All three layers are closely related to one another and only their interplay can result in a successful knowledge network that creates value for its company. The following illustration shows the reference model as a whole by illustrating its three interrelated layers: the relationship with the company environment (facilitating conditions), the process within the network (knowledge work processes) and the supporting tools with which to create the appropriate environment within the network, as well as with which to support its processes (knowledge network architecture).

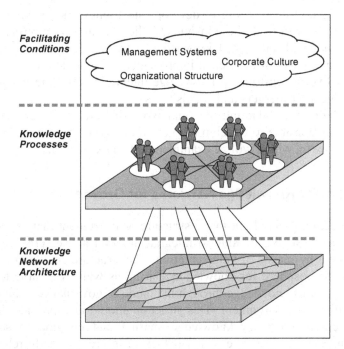

Fig. 1.2 Reference model of a Knowledge Network and its interrelated layers (Source: Back et al., 2005)

To summarize the arguments of this section: one major result of our research is that knowledge networks can support managed knowledge sharing and creation better than other organizational forms due to their specific network structure in combination with their task orientation and management ability. One important characteristic of all organizational forms that needs to be highlighted as a major advantage is that these forms can not be imitated. This is because the members' tacit knowledge and their sharing thereof are individually determined and related to the facilitating conditions of their surroundings. Knowledge networks are more focused on knowledge sharing and creation, which allows them to support innovation better than the other forms described above. Therefore, networks seem to contain all the necessary attributes and inherent potential to improve value innovation through an internal and external growth strategy.

Now we need to raise the question whether the knowledge network framework can be adapted to follow an internal and/or external growth strategy. How robust are the components of the framework? Which components need to be changed? And prior to all three questions: Are the components to be adapted in order to follow a growth strategy always the same? Is it therefore possible to develop one framework for knowledge networks for growth from these insights? Following an action research approach we adapted and tested knowledge networks for growth in three companies in respect of the fields: improvement of innovation through innovation networks, customers' knowledge integration, and the integration of knowledge after mergers and acquisitions.

By validating and adapting the framework of intra-organizational networks, it was possible to develop the new framework for knowledge networks for growth, which will be examined in the next section.

Framework for Knowledge Networks for Growth

The introduction pointed out that a structure or instrument that supports a growth strategy should be able to integrate internal and external sources and link them by means of value creation. The structure should create the appropriate atmosphere for knowledge sharing as well as be able to support integration of knowledge through the mode of governance, which creates a facilitating environment. This structure should also provide the appropriate environment for knowledge sharing and creation to support innovation. Such an instrument can, if located in areas directly related to company growth, support the strategy of profitable growth. By adapting certain components, the knowledge networks framework could be the required instrument with which to support company growth.

In summary, the network structure enables the integration of dispersed people, can create the appropriate atmosphere to enable knowledge creation and can directly support business goals related to company growth. Consequently, knowledge networks, modified to consistently follow a growth strategy, can support knowledge sharing and creation which will improve internal innovation and ease the knowledge integration after M&A. Both ways will lead to sustained, profitable growth through value innovation and will therefore shape the conditions of the industry.

Methodology

The results presented in this section are derived from an action research approach followed by the research center KnowledgeSource[2] (Back et. al, 2005). The results were formulated after data had been collected at partnering companies, the concept of knowledge networks had been adapted to that of knowledge networks for growth and the concept had been jointly developed with, tested and implemented in the partnering companies[3]. For the adaptation of the initial framework, multiple sources of evidence, such as internal company documents and archival data, intranet resources as well as publicly available information, were used.

To collect detailed information about the fields in which such a network should be implemented, a theoretical framework for knowledge networks for growth was developed in the selected fields by combining theoretical insights from a broad literature review with the collected information from the data sources described above. The identified gaps in this theoretical framework were explained and the fine-tuning to accommodate the purpose and members of a specific network was done by collecting and analyzing semi-structured interviews with potential network members, stakeholders and shareholders. To complete the data collection, direct and participant observation techniques were used during site visits pertaining to the individual implementations. E.g., to develop a knowledge network supporting innovation through the integration of customer knowledge, we first delved into the theory to identify crucial factors that require adaptation when integrating customers.

Through empirical studies we learned that it is important to identify the appropriate customer in respect of the network's purpose. Representatives of customer groups seem to be better able to create incremental innovation, and improvement of existing service processes or products, while visionary customers also seem able to support radical innovation with their out-of-the-box thinking.

---

[2] The results presented in this article were gained in the two-year research project "Competence Center Knowledge Networks for Growth", which is part of the University of St. Gallen's research center, KnowledgeSource (for more information, see www.knowledgesource.org). The authors wish to thank research assistants Grzegorz Gurgul and Maria Rumyantseva who were an indispensable part of the research project.

[3] The authors also wish to thank the corporate members of the partnering companies: Hewlett Packard GmbH, Unilever N.V. and RWE Net were all full members of the research team and were crucially important for the results gained and the applicability of the framework in practice.

After adapting the necessary factors in the framework for knowledge networks to meet the challenge to integrate customers, the theoretical framework was discussed with the partner companies in workshops in order to adapt and make it more useful in practice. E.g., our partnering companies told us that it is not difficult to convince individual customers to share their knowledge, but the company behind the customer, if its customers are not end consumers but companies in a value chain. Besides creating individual and corporate value, value for the customer's company also plays a crucial role in motivating cooperation.

In the next step, the more practical framework was adapted for implementation and tested in a company. This meant that company-specific factors, such as its corporate culture and structure, its existing information and communication systems, or its range of frequently used tools, were taken into account to adapt the framework to a specific company and its specific purpose. This "third" adaptation was done by collecting data through interviews, documents, questionnaires and observation, in fact, whatever was necessary to apply the framework to the business need of the individual company.

After setting up the network within the company, additional data were collected to refine the network and improve its action. After an appropriate period of time the findings were discussed in workshops with all the company representative in order to isolate company-specific factors and to identify general factors that need to be adapted for all companies. The framework – first tested and then generalized – is an example of a knowledge network for growth.

Based on an investigation of companies' practices and by using the existing and adapted knowledge network methodology as a point of departure, a framework for knowledge networks for growth is suggested and briefly described in the following section.

Knowledge Networks for Growth in Practice: Following an Internal Strategy through Innovation

Knowledge networks are successful at focusing on knowledge sharing and creation between subject matter experts because they help to create synergies between and reduce the development of redundancies in the different business units and departments of a company. It seems that companies' knowledge-sharing activities are becoming more focused on areas where these activities are needed, instead of on company-wide knowledge sharing through the intranet and an information push. As mentioned before, integrating external knowledge sources can lead to huge advantages for knowledge creation and innovation. The knowledge sources with which to enrich the internal innovation process can be customer or other independent business groups. With both groups similar problems, such as different cultures that need to be combined, a strong focus on individual and business groups or the customer company's values, and different information and communication systems, to name only a few, occur.

Because the network structure enables individuals or whole organizations to be connected without restructuring the organization, it enables the integration of external sources. Since the network activities occupy only a limited number of the monthly working hours, the single members gain some value by being both closely connected with their daily business and having links with the main organization. They could meet once a month and share their knowledge of a certain task, such as a support process, and devise plans to improve it. It is therefore important that the task on which they work should not only be personally motivating, but also be motivating for their companies.

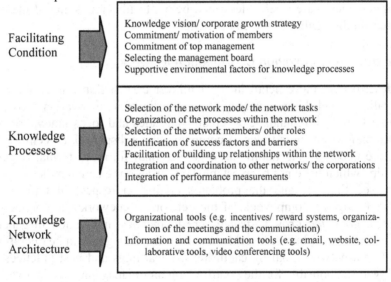

Fig. 1.3 Detailing the framework for knowledge networks for growth

Since there are, however, differences between integrating customers and supporting cooperation between independent business units, both types of knowledge networks for growth are described individually according to the main components (the right column in the figure above) of the framework, as identified by our research.

Figure 1.3 shows a more detailed framework for knowledge networks for growth, where the three interlinked layers are specified in a number of components that each layer summarizes. These components are similar for intra-organizational networks, networks that connect knowledge owners within the same company in order to support the transfer of knowledge as well as for knowledge networks for growth where external sources of knowledge are also linked in order to support innovation by means of facilitating the transfer and creation of knowledge. Although the components are similar, it is the quality of each component that makes the difference. As briefly described in the example above, a component such as *the motivation of the members* (within the first layer) needs to be addressed differently in a customer integration network (how do we motivate our customers to share their knowledge?) than in an innovation coordination network (how do we motivate portfolio managers from different, independent business or product groups to share knowledge and cooperate?). These two networks – both aiming to support internal innovation but through different approaches – are briefly described below to illustrate some of the differences in the quality of the components.

Example of an Innovation Coordination Network

As described in more detail in the Unilever case within this book, on a generalized level the company aims to coordinate its innovation activities in order to reduce redundancies, create synergies and focus innovation activities on new business fields. A company with a dispersed, de-centralized structure needs to add additional organizational forms to formalize relationships which have not been established through the company's structure itself (see Fig. 1.1 and the problems arising in respect of knowledge flows). Using the components of the network framework, the company's *strategic goal and growth strategy* are to increase innovation in general and in certain new business fields in particular. This goal can be operationalized as a network goal by capturing the learnings and best practices of employees responsible for the coordination and management of innovation projects within the single business groups. The network's members therefore need to be portfolio managers of innovation projects of the different groups or their employees.

The discussion of the component *motivation of members and top management* can serve to answer which are the right members. The individuals in the networks will be motivated when they exchange knowledge that also supports their daily work. E.g., best practices on how to manage projects that are not in line with the innovation process requirements, or the coordination of projects involving top management from different departments.

All members therefore need to have the same working background and experience in order to create individual value through knowledge exchange. The top management's motivation can be excited by creating corporate value. Only if the members are empowered to integrate the best practices and lessons learned have been discussed can innovation project cycles be shortened and will the number of successfully launched projects be increased.

On a higher corporate level the coordination of innovation projects across business groups will save costs and help to focus innovation activities on new and promising business fields. To ensure that the network achieves these proposed values, a *management board* consisting of the higher management of the different business groups involved should meet frequently to monitor the results. Because it is difficult to coordinate top management's time, existing regular meetings, like the monthly innovation directors' meeting, should be used to discuss the network results. This board should not only act as an advisory board, but should also decide on environmental factors that support the network, such as the budget for regular face-to-face meetings of network members, or whether a new, electronic innovation process management – already successfully established in one business group – should be integrated into all the business groups to support the network by creating transparency etc.

In the next layer of the processes, the *network's task* is already clear: the portfolio managers should frequently gather in order to identify best practices and lessons learned, to discuss current and future innovation activities in order to reduce redundancies and – in the best case – to coordinate their innovation activities to better focus on new and promising business fields. Although this clearly defined communication by the network obviously results in certain *knowledge processes*, such as knowledge sharing and the creation of existing and new projects, the precondition is capturing and accessing existing knowledge on innovation activities in the different business groups. The close *link to the business process*, innovation, is realized through the network members' function in their business group and through their empowerment to integrate network results in their business processes.

The *members' roles* as representatives of their business group seem to be clear, but the important role of the *network leader* has not yet been clarified. Network members are facilitated by a network leader who, in turn, is directed by a board of managers. The network leader should help to create a positive and knowledge-friendly atmosphere that supports the processes and helps to build trust. The network leader is responsible for organizing the working processes and integrating tools that are regarded as helpful to all the participants. In order to serve as a neutral moderator and organizer of the network, its leader should not be one of the members nor be from higher management. In the best case it should be a person known and trusted by all members and experienced with the company's innovation process to help the network identify best practices and lessons learned. Therefore, besides having strong social capabilities in order to balance the powerful business groups members and to create a less competitive environment, the network leader's selection is an important success factor for this network.

Other success factors are a good *performance measurement* to illustrate the value that the network creates which, in turn, helps to support the management's commitment and helps the leader to monitor the network in order to identify areas of improvement. Because the main goal of the network is to reduce redundancies and create synergies, it seems obvious that the network needs to be linked with other networks in related areas and functions responsible for managing corporate venture, outsourcing or scanning.

The last layer describes the *tools* that are helpful in creating the appropriate environment and that support the process within the network. For the innovation coordination network, transparency regarding the status of innovation activities seems crucial. Information and communication technology (ICT) tools provide electronic help in creating this transparency. To enable all members to use such management tools between meetings as well, the electronic systems needs to be linked with the systems of the business units involved. Other organizational tools, such as frequent face-to-face meetings, or pleasant meeting rooms, as well as other information and communication tools with which to store explicit knowledge like patents, project documents etc. in databases, or with which to send email – as virtual communication – in the periods between the personal meetings, are necessary for smooth cooperation.

By linking all these components together, the blueprint for an innovation coordination network is produced and needs to be adapted in respect of the company specifics. The methodology, described later in this book, helps management to apply this blueprint and build a successful knowledge network for growth.

The Unilever case to be found in this book further illustrates a customer integration network in practice.

Example of a Customer Integration Network

From a corporate perspective, integrating customers' tacit knowledge through a knowledge network includes the *vision* that customers own knowledge which is valuable for corporate innovation, whether incremental or radical. To combine employees and customers in order to share and create knowledge within a network seems to be a good approach. However, there are some obstacles to consider. Which customers possess the right knowledge and how does one motivate them to share their knowledge in order to increase the services and products for which they have to pay, are only two of the obstacles to overcome.

Customers, like employees, will only share their knowledge if *motivated* through personal values. These values might be to exchange knowledge with other customers experiencing the same problems and to try to solve these problems with the help of the corporate experts. In the process, the company will learn more about customer demands, and the customers will solve their problems and produce a better practice. If the customers are not end consumers but companies, it is necessary to not only obtain individual members but also their management's commitment. Customers, like employees, normally have no say regarding their involvement in long-term activities with other companies without their management's approval. To increase commitment, the network needs to create value for the individual companies represented. Products and services that are more customer oriented, are not exclusively valuable to the companies involved in the network because these products and serves will be made available to the public in order to make a profit. However, being involved in the development of a future product or service strategy helps companies to decide their own strategy, since this is then based on more information than they had before. If such an involvement has other financial advantages, this too can help to increase motivation. Companies that aim to integrate their customers into the innovation process should act extremely carefully because they might doubly fail if their network activity fails: their innovation activity will fail and they might lose their customers.

A *management board* comprised of managers of all the companies supporting and advising the networks can be a crucial success factor. Another *supportive factor* is the appropriate environment for the network meetings, the right frequency of such meeting and a strong support of virtual communication. The members of a customer integration network are geographically dispersed, and live in different company cultures and structures, which lead to stronger demands to create an independent, supporting environment through agreeable locations, and high recognition of the network's activities and tools, especially information and communication tools that can be easily linked with all the involved companies.

Taking the network process layer into consideration, the *task of the network* needs to focus on knowledge creation from a knowledge perspective and on improving existing or creating new services or products from a business process perspective. To facilitate customer-members' commitment, the focus should be on processes and services that directly improve the customer's work.

Returning to the questions raised above on how to *select the customers* with the right knowledge, it is clear that this cannot be easily answered. If a company wishes to discuss radical ideas, lead users or very creative customers are needed, but if the outcome of the network should serve a special customer group, the network needs customers from this group. Generally, marketing, sales or support departments know which customers fulfil those needs. To ease customers' integration into the network, corporate employees who have worked with them before should be integrated in the network as well. The network leader should work out *network processes* that fit the working structure of the corporate members as well as the customer-members within the network. The processes should also include time to build relationships between the customers, because the exchange of common practices and the building of further working relationships between the customers can be an additional value for them that could motivate participation. Examples of *performance measures* can be the number of ideas discussed and worked out as proposals, or the number of innovation projects drafted and started.

As far as the third layer – the *tools* – is concerned, the mentioned ability to integrate is mandatory. Especially the information and communication tools should have the ability to integrate with corporate and customer systems. Collaborative tools, like discussion platforms or an on-line chat tool, support communication between face-to-face meetings. Such support might be necessary because the different management systems and different timetables might make it more difficult to find opportunities to meet that suit everybody.

The Hewlett Packard case later in this book further illustrates a customer integration network in practice.

Knowledge Networks for Growth in Practice: Following an External Strategy through M&A

The ideal M&A scenario is one where there is no loser or winner, but a totally new company that will lead to a competitive advantage that none of the single entities could have achieved.

Research on post-merger integration experience has revealed that collaborative problem-solving workshops help to reduce inter-group conflicts and misperceptions. This is especially helpful when having to deal with employees from formerly different companies and, currently, even from different cultures. To overcome the barriers between people, they need to interact with one another. A knowledge network, as an organizational structure that spans hierarchies as well as geographical, structural and merger-related barriers, and which is supported by the management, will help to support the integration process and will lead to the creation of new social ties.

Example of a Knowledge Integration after M&A Network

Picturing a network which integrates knowledge after a merger or acquisition, according to the components of the reference model, the *growth strategy* followed is to grow by acquiring external knowledge. But synergies can only be realized when both companies cooperate and link their knowledge in order to create a new and better entity. The integration of technology, structures and people in order to transfer existing and create new knowledge, is mandatory. But the organizational changes and the uncertainty associated with the merger or the acquisition form natural barriers to knowledge sharing and integration. Therefore, the component *motivation and commitment of the members* becomes crucially important.

In the merger and acquisition process, the network serves as an intermediate entity to link up a small number of people from both parties in order to create something new. By doing so they also illustrate that the integration of knowledge (and companies) makes sense from an individual and a corporate perspective. But illustrating the personal and corporate value before network action has been realized, is not an easy task at all. The value can be realized through the *selection of the network task*, which should create a new internal process, service or product that requires important knowledge from both companies.

The *selection of members and their recognition* as experts of a knowledge domain in both companies – the visibility that is associated with this also provides some certainty of retaining a job in the newly merged company – and the knowledge gained through the exchange between members will be personally valuable to them. Consequently, this will support their *commitment*. But to overcome the fears of losing a job, the uncertainty caused by the organizational changes and individual competition, the network needs to create trust between the individual members. This is an essential precondition and can be achieved over time through successful cooperation. This network might therefore need to pay more attention to building its own supportive culture, and might have to be more independent of the unsettling corporate environment than the other examples of networks in growth areas.

Management's commitment is easier to obtain than the members' commitment because the network will be built up in a post-merger phase when the organizational changes have occurred and the management decisions have already been taken. The uncertainty on the management level is therefore less, but the structures are new and need to be routinized over time. Management wants to see proof of the value that the merger promised and the network might remain under strong pressure to realize this value as its first cooperative activity. Consequently, the network can be regarded as a test of whether the merger or acquisition has been successfully realized and has reached it promised value by creating synergies.

The *management board* should consist of the members' management as well as of the integration managers who supervise and support all integration activities. The board should support the network's activities and communicate its first results as a merger or acquisition success on a corporate level. To *motivate* further cooperation for knowledge integration, the network's activities should be visible, e.g., through a website presence or by featuring in the company news.

As previously mentioned, on a process level the *network task* plays a crucial role and needs to be selected very carefully. Since the first test of cooperation that is realized in the network needs to be successfully concluded, the network goal should aim to create a mixture of quick and easy wins and long-term goals. Creating new customer services that could only have been created after the merger might be an appropriate long-term goal. Improving existing services through the learnings gained in the two companies might be an appropriate short-term goal. Another short-term goal could be to formulate best practices in the knowledge domain of the network and to publish them on the website in order to create value for employees outside the network as well.

It is valuable to first capture and discuss all the knowledge that exists in both companies. One of the network leader's major tasks will therefore be to create an atmosphere within the network in which discussions of the company's knowledge and people is not colored by false "old" company loyalty. Consequently, the leader should be a recognized expert with great social skills in order to manage such a network under management pressure.

The second phase of the network activities should be the discussion and selection of the process or products that need to be improved or developed first. Also the mentioned balances between short- and long-term activities should play a role when selecting the network tasks. The selection of the detailed *network tasks* should be a team effort in order to increase trust and cooperation in the network. Beside the tasks, the *selection of the right members* is important to achieve the first integration successes. The members should be recognized experts from both companies, but should also be open-minded in order to overcome the obstacles raised by the merger.

Although the integration managers are already part of the management board, they also should participate in the network meetings in order to *link the network's activities* with the other integration activities in the company and communicate its results to the appropriate parts of the company. Setting up a *performance measure* is mandatory for a network whose success might communicate the success or failure of the entire merger or acquisition. These measures should mainly help the network leader and the management board to monitor the network's activities in order to reduce the risk of failure.

As far as the last layer – *tools* – is concerned, the visibility of the network's activities and communication of its success could be realized by a website available on the company's intranet. Since the network is a post-merger activity that occurs after the technical and organizational integration, the compatibility of the systems should already be known. The organizational tools, like a supportive meeting environment or the visibility and recognition of the members as experts through active communication, are more important in this network than the supportive aspects of the ICT tools (for the transfer of documented, explicit knowledge). Network meetings that provide an opportunity for the sharing of tacit knowledge and for documenting it as explicit knowledge should therefore occur frequently.

An example from practice illustrating a network that supports growth through successful knowledge integration after merger and acquisition, is the RWE network case study in this book.

General Factors to Be Adapted for Knowledge Networks for Growth

To summarize the results illustrated before, when comparing the components and their qualities it becomes obvious that knowledge networks in growth areas depend on the same components. By comparing the three knowledge networks for growth as described above, we can create one framework for knowledge networks for growth in which certain components are more important for success and failure than others. These components are highlighted in the figure 1.4 and briefly described.

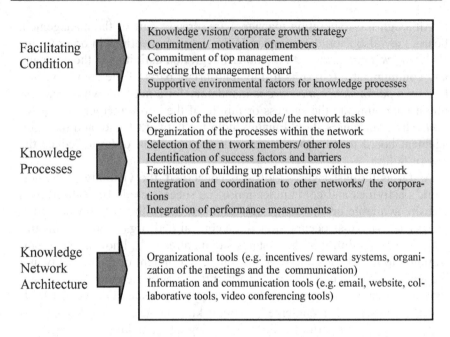

Fig. 1.4 Knowledge Networks for Growth Framework and Methodology

To summarize, on the level of *facilitating conditions* all networks need to have an explicit corporate growth strategy with which to fulfil the company's vision of growth through certain activities. The network goals need to be directly translated from the corporate growth strategy into knowledge and operative goals to follow. Because activities in growth areas are obviously under more management pressure, but are also more risky, the members' commitment and motivation are crucial for the network's success. All the cases illustrate that motivation can be increased through activities largely connected to recognition as well as the network task selection, which should create value for the company as well as for the individual member. All the investigated networks need to overcome certain obstacles connected to the growth areas that require support. Not all of them can be influenced directly, but it helps to illustrate possible or existing barriers and to discuss them openly within the network and its management board. But in all networks a knowledge-friendly atmosphere of trust and recognition is mandatory to provide the appropriate environment for the network action.

On the *process layer*, the link between the network processes and the business process needs to be direct in order to create the proposed support for the company's growth strategy. This link can be realized through the

network goals as well as through the integration of other company functions, such as those of the integration manager or the sales representative,
within the network. Linking the network action with other initiatives, e.g.,
integration initiatives in the post-merger phase, or innovation activities in
other regional centers and the rest of the company, will support the knowledge flow and prevent the network from becoming isolated. Since networks set up in growth areas are likely to fail because of the many barriers
that they need to overcome, their monitoring and constant improvement
are important. Therefore, the right performance measurement and a very
sensible communication of results or expectations are mandatory for success. Consequently, we have developed a new integrated measurement system for knowledge networks as is illustrated in the performance measurement article in this book.

The *architectural layer* of the proposed framework includes factors such
as frequent face-to-face meetings to build trust and share tacit knowledge
as well as ICT tools with which to communicate virtually and to support
the storage and transfer of explicit knowledge.

Our research not only identified the components and their qualities for
knowledge networks to support growth areas, but also the fact that all
components need to be adapted to the company specifics in order to work
well. These adaptations are mandatory, but not easy to achieve. By transforming the components into a process, we were able to develop a methodology for setting up the components, with links and tools to help companies identify where and how to apply the component for their needs (for
details see the methodology section in this book).

Discussion and Conclusion

This study is an attempt to address the concept of knowledge networks that
can support company growth, thus answering the research question: how
can knowledge networks support internal and external growth?

The proposed framework is based on the reference model for knowledge
networks and has been adapted in respect of the requirements of the theory
of innovation and M&A. The framework for knowledge networks has been
tested in the three fields of customer knowledge integration, namely the integration of external knowledge sources, internal innovation and knowledge integration in the post-merger phase. We tested knowledge networks

for growth by adapting the framework for companies[4], and consequently deducing the general factors to be adapted in all the networks. We argue that by adjusting these factors it is also possible to adapt the knowledge network framework for other growth areas.

The results of this study have major implications. First, that knowledge networks can be used to directly support a strategic goal like company growth. Second, that the framework of intra-organizational knowledge networks needs to be adapted.

This study does, however, have limitations. The framework of knowledge networks for growth has only been implemented and tested in three companies and in three different fields: customer knowledge integration, internal innovation support and post-merger integration. The limited sample and the limited fields of implementation restrict the range of results that can be drawn for generalization. There are more areas where company growth can be supported and there is clearly a need to implement and test the framework in a wider range of companies. However, the findings of this study are on a par with studies that describe the value of knowledge integration and creation in supporting company growth in different contexts, which may have extended the generalizability of research in this area.

This study also offers several directions for future research. In particular, the development of a methodology for adapting and setting up knowledge networks for growth to offer companies the possibility of using the approach and scientists the opportunity to study and validate the results. Another way to triangulate these issues would be to investigate knowledge networks in practices that support areas related to company growth, but are not meant to do so explicitly. In another promising area of research, a distinction can be made between research on innovation and that on post-merger integration in general. More requirements should be identified and consequently used to fine-tune the proposed framework. In addition, future studies may wish to explore the potentials of other organizational forms, such as communities of practice or project teams, to support company growth. These studies can be modeled on the understanding of the influence that organizational forms have on the support of important strategic goals.

In summary, this article extends our understanding of knowledge networks for growth. It extends the results of existing research by using the requirements from theory to create the framework and by testing the model in three companies, which will be illustrated in more detail in the follow-

---

[4] See the methodology section of this article

ing cases. The results strongly support the proposed knowledge network for growth model and suggest several useful areas for future research.

2 Supporting Integration after M&A through Knowledge Networks within RWE Net

Grzegorz Gurgul[1], Ellen Enkel[1], Kordula Schulte[2] and Carl-Heinrich Kruse[2]

[1]Research Center KnowledgeSource, University of St. Gallen, Switzerland
[2]RWE Net

Abstract

After a hundred years of market control in Germany, the electricity market is currently characterized by partial market deregulation and, consequently, the utilities have to cope with increased competition. To remain competitive, a major growth factor can be stimulated through mergers and acquisitions (M&A) that encourage synergies as well as providing access to new geographical areas. The companies RWE AG[5] and VEW AG[6] followed this path to growth and merged. After the merger both companies were reorganized and divided into several business units.

The challenge of a merged company is to overcome the barriers related to a merger and bring together the employees in order to formalize a knowledge transfer in the relevant strategic business fields. This process is called "Knowledge Integration after M&A". To implement the process, the company needs a comprehensive tool with which to integrate its employees' knowledge. The goal of the project was to test the MERLIN methodology that had been established for intra-organizational knowledge networks in a new business field, adapt it for the new field of use, implement the knowledge network, and accompany it during the set-up phase.

The background to this case study describes RWE Net's historical background and the urgency with which a formalized knowledge transfer was

---

[5] RWE: Rheinisch-Westfälische Elektrizitätswerke, also called RWE Group
[6] VEW: Vereinigte Elektrizitätswerke Westfalen, also called VEW Group

undertaken. Thereafter the approach – the various steps of a knowledge network setup – is described. This is followed by conclusions regarding a network's developmental steps. The case is concluded with the lessons learned and the most important general recommendations.

Knowledge Integration after M&A in RWE Net

Conceptual Background

Mergers and acquisitions (M&A) provide an opportunity to gain growth and are a means through which to extend a company's workforce, internal abilities, and product range within a short time. M&A are not new phenomena, the first boom in mergers and acquisitions having occurred at the end of the 19th century. The rate at which M&A fail indicates that many problems pertaining to post-merger integration management[7] are still unsolved, with some researchers even considering mergers and acquisitions a license to kill companies (Jansen, 2002). Acquiring and merging firms have indeed led to the discovery that the transfer and utilization of knowledge through these means can be a difficult task. This transfer and utilization of knowledge is contingent upon the successful integration of the acquired or merged unit – a process that very often fails outright. And although knowledge management has gained significance within the field of management and in academia since the nineties, it has almost no significance within the field of mergers and acquisitions.

The post-merger integration phase is characterized by the disarray of nearly all routines, as well as all communication and decision procedures in the relevant business. A merger or an acquisition generally entails reorganization during the integration of the two companies, but huge mergers of equals tend to change an organization fundamentally. During the reorganization, employees' social networks are destroyed, ways of knowledge sharing and exchanging experiences are severed through the creation of new business units, layoffs and the early retirement of employees. Mergers and acquisitions are furthermore likely to lead to the destruction of intellectual and social capital, e.g., after a merger or acquisition the staff turnover rate increases significantly, with the best people generally leaving voluntarily and first (Kay and Shelton, 2000). Post-merger integration

---

[7] Merger and acquisition processes are divided into three sequential steps: searching for the right target, realization of the due diligence, and integration of the merged or acquired company (Haspelagh and Jemison, 1991).

measures also tend to be too brief to induce implicit knowledge transfer as well as not focusing on the efficient transfer of implicit knowledge at all.

Critical factors that could influence decisions relating to customer relationship, experience of new methods of implementation, and work approaches are examples of the knowledge that often remains undocumented, or is lost during post-merger integration. There are further risks related to lost knowledge that could also be failure factors in the knowledge integration process after mergers or acquisitions. One of these is the announcement of a merger or acquisition itself. Such an announcement creates organizational stress, and employees then tend to become reluctant to share their knowledge, since they suddenly appear to become aware of risks related to losing their job, induced by a fear of not being distinguishable from others if their knowledge and experience were to be shared (cf. Probst and Knaese, 1999). These knowledge risks take the form of employees' mistrust of the merger or acquisition, problems of scope caused by their new range of tasks, and power conflicts between employees contemplating their future. When the situation also involves prejudices against the employees of the merged or acquired company, employees are inclined to remain in their newly detruncated social networks, resulting in a poor transfer of knowledge (cf. Empson, 2001).

In order to overcome the shortcomings of the usual integration approaches, knowledge management approaches have to be taken into account before and after the M&A (Connolly and Klein, 2002; North and Blanco, 2003). The knowledge management initiatives can be differentiated according to the time that has elapsed since the M&A idea and when the deal was sealed (see figure 2.1). In the pre-merger phase, transitions groups in cooperation with the knowledge managers in each company accumulate the overall M&A activities, which include, e.g., the knowledge of customer relationships, suppliers, and experts. This accumulated knowledge is debriefed after the two companies become one entity in order to speed the integration process, to communicate with the relevant knowledge carriers and to act in a trustworthy manner.

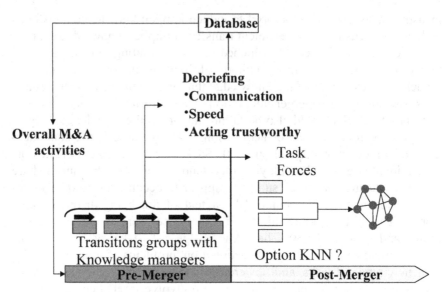

Fig. 2.1 KM initiatives' time allotment

The short-term, post-merger integration phase is characterized by two issues: an increase in stress and uncertainty among employees, and, simultaneously, the technical and organizational integration of the two companies. In this early phase of the integration task, task forces are the appropriate form for knowledge management initiatives and are responsible for the technical and operational integration. They are additionally mainly responsible for the integration of explicit knowledge as is found in repositories of knowledge carriers, and completed projects. In order not to lose the knowledge acquired during this stage of the integration, the knowledge managers have to be consistently involved in the processes and therefore play the role of knowledge accumulators.

At the end of the technical and organizational integration, the company has to choose further knowledge management initiatives, i.e. on the basis of the work done by the task forces, the choice of a knowledge network or another organizational form for further post-merger knowledge integration has to be made. The choice of a knowledge network option should be based on the fact whether there are still barriers and separate knowledge bases within the company and whether they resist integration efforts. A knowledge network is an effective instrument with which to connect knowledge owners that are disconnected after reorganization and, through its specific network structure, facilitates the transfer of implicit knowledge. Also in the long-term, post-merger phase the knowledge network organizational form is the most appropriate initiative for the transfer of implicit knowledge. A well-established knowledge network provides an appropriate atmosphere through its facilitating conditions, processes and infrastructure.

The importance of the implicit knowledge embedded in people's minds requires that, besides focusing on the integration of technical systems, an integration approach be chosen which will integrate employees' knowledge and attempt to overcome merger-related barriers. Research on post-merger integration experiences has revealed that the achievement of a successful acquisition in terms of R&D performance depends on both a high level of human integration and task integration. A cautious and an effective approach to a successful acquisition concentrates on a human integration, which leads to a shared identity and mutual respect, and entails synergies based on knowledge sharing and application (Birkinshaw et al., 2000). The aftermath of the merger or acquisition not only requires a centralized integration architecture, in which the technical and organizational integration will be carried out, but also decentralized integration architecture, e.g., communities of practice and knowledge networks. An organizational structure that spans hierarchies as well as geographical-, structural- and merger-related barriers is needed. Such an organizational structure would unite geographically dispersed employees and create new social ties. During face-to-face meetings participants could then exchange experiences and abolish prejudices related to the merger.

Approach Taken by the Research Project

Based on the initial situation, the goal was to create a framework that would support the knowledge and cultural integration of the employees, and ensure knowledge transfer between the regional centers and business units. The main task of the research project was to test the existing MERLIN methodology in a new business field, since the methodology was established for intra-organizational knowledge networks. The research question was: How to adapt the existing MERLIN methodology to the new field of knowledge integration after M&A? In order to ensure the usefulness of the outcome for all person involved, the research project was carried out by representatives of RWE Net and the research center, cooperating closely.

The newness and complexity of the real life problem suggested a qualitative research approach. The investigations were based on four pillars:

- a study of the recent literature on the topic of knowledge management and M&A,

- a study of the company's internal documentation,
- semi-structured interviews and
- a participant observation.

The documentation study contributed to the understanding of the company's integration approaches and historical issues. The literature study enabled the generation of a mental framework that, superimposed on the company's specific situation, served as a basis for the subsequent interviews. The semi-structured interviews provided in-depth experience and new insights into the company's internal situation (Cohen et al., 2000), p. 268 ff.). The semi-structured nature of the interviews allowed the statements to be analyzed and compared more easily (Kvale, 1996), p. 187 ff.). The interviews were conducted with eleven RWE Net representatives over a two-month period in 2002. The participant observation was carried out during the kick-off workshop in late 2002 and contributed to the understanding of the significance of establishing social ties in a late post-merger integration phase.

Historical Background

The historical roots of the RWE Group date back to the 19th century, to the beginning of electrification and industrialization in Germany. RWE Group's first decades are closely linked to the growth of the Ruhr basin and its steelworks, the electrification of German cities, and the country's captains of industry, such as Thyssen and Stinnes. Apart from electricity production and transmission, the RWE Group diversified into water supply, waste management, and telecommunication, and invested in the building and printing industry during the 20th century. In 1990, RWE Group was reorganized into divisions ("Unternehmensbereiche"), with the largest – focusing on electricity production and distribution – being led by RWE Energie.

RWE Group's development in the last decade of the 20th century faced one major challenge: the European Union electricity market, formerly state regulated, was partially deregulated in April 1998. The RWE Group was confronted with a different, difficult, and challenging situation in the new non-regulated market. On the one hand, RWE Group had to act in a free market and cope with competition, but, on the other hand, the non-regulated market presented a growth opportunity. The energy market liberalization caused a radical change in the competitive environment and led to consolidation of the utilities. While there had been eight nation-wide utilities in Germany before the liberalization, afterwards only five larger utilities remained.

In 1998 and 1999, the RWE Group and the VEW Group had to find a merger partner to face the challenges of the partial deregulation of the electricity market and the increasing competition. The geographical proximity of the two headquarters and the proximity of their business finally clinched the matter. In 2000, the Federal Cartel Office agreed to the merger. This entailed a huge reorganization of the two companies. Five subsidiaries were created from the two antecedent companies with all RWE Energie and VEW Energie's[8] activities related to the power grid in Germany being bundled in RWE Net.

Currently RWE Net employs about 6,000 people, has a grid area of 36,800 km^2 in the western part of Germany, and a turnover of €3,7 billion. RWE Net's task is the supply security, i.e. focusing on the electricity network activities of the RWE Group, all functions concerning grid design, construction, and operation. RWE Net has a decentralized structure with 13 regional centers responsible for the above-mentioned activities in their regions in order to be represented locally. In turn, the 13 regional centers are incorporated into two larger regional centers, "Region Nord" (Northern Region) and "Region Süd" (Southern Region), which reflect RWE Net's geographical limits. Another important task is the surveillance and control of the ultra-high voltage system for the northern part of Central Europe.

The Demand for Knowledge Integration after M&A

Immediately after the merger, the integration of the grid activities of RWE Energie and VEW Energie into the new RWE Net, took place. During the following two years the integration managers and the responsible project teams carried out a thorough technical and organizational integration of the companies, which resulted in a complete reorganization of the whole company. However, the integration measures did not include a formal knowledge transfer between the regional centers, although the relevant employees had worked on the same tasks and had faced similar problems. But there were also barriers – strongly related to the merger – which persisted during the two-year integration endeavor. These included cultural misunderstandings as well as physical and mental signs of the former companies. The geographical- and merger-related barriers led to the continuation of

---

[8] VEW Energie was a division of VEW dealing with electricity production and distribution and gas supply.

separate knowledge bases within the company. The barriers inhibited the realization of the intended knowledge synergies.

One of RWE Net's businesses is street lighting[9] – a business field that affects all regional centers in which employees face similar problems. Thus these employees require a collective knowledge base in order to learn and to gain strategic advantage despite the fact that the provision of street lighting had been led differently in the two former companies. VEW Energie had had a central department responsible for the street lighting in their area and in which all the experts in the field of street lighting were brought together. RWE Energie's experts, on the other hand, had been decentralized, each regional center having its own experts on street lighting.

It was crucial that RWE Net should have a common approach, since the significance of the provision of street lighting is that it serves as a door opener for further businesses with the municipalities. Furthermore, street lighting is a deregulated business activity in which all utilities compete against one another and from which municipalities can choose their electricity supplier. However, this field of business activity demands sustained contact with the customers. A close relationship with municipalities is highly significant for the company's future business, since many of the concessionary contracts, regulating the laying of electricity lines on public property, will expire in 2006. If a utility company can prove its reliability through its work performance and create a social network with the representatives of a municipality, it can facilitate the negotiation of the new concessionary contracts, since it is easier to extend an existing contract than change to a new service provider. During interaction with the municipalities and with the challenges of street lighting, the RWE Net representatives gained implicit knowledge that was often not documented.

This situation called for the urgent formalization of the transfer of knowledge between geographically dispersed employees working in the same field. The most obvious means of achieving this was to bring the people together in order to overcome the geographical and merger-related barriers. It is therefore crucial that RWE Net's representatives responsible for a municipality in each of the company's regional centers share their experience of the treatment of the municipality representatives. Besides the obvious goal of knowledge sharing, the underlying goal of the knowledge

---

[9] Street lighting is currently taken for granted: facilitating everyone's life, the smooth flow of traffic, and turning night into day. Furthermore, illumination provides security, and is so much part of our quality of life that we do not realize its importance, or the knowledge required to have it until it is not available. The provision of street lighting alone demands tacit knowledge of the appropriate luminosity related to traffic density, as well as knowledge of glare limitation.

network ought to provide the employees from the formerly different companies with a sense of community and belonging.

The Development of an M&A Integration Network

Finding the Appropriate Structure for Knowledge Integration

Isolated knowledge islands had remained within the merged company,
RWE Net, due to its structural dispersion and merger-related barriers. A
knowledge management initiative within RWE Net had to cover these
problems in three regional centers and several business units. Research on
post-merger integration experience also revealed that collaborative problem-solving workshops help to reduce inter-group conflicts and misperceptions when dealing with employees from formerly different companies
who still adhere to their different cultures (Buono and Bowditch, 1989, p.
206 ff.). Thus, barriers between people can also only be overcome if they
interact with one another. A decentralized integration architecture, span-
ning hierarchies, geographical and structural barriers, and supported by
ICT tools as well as management, would provide a solution (Morosini et
al., 1998).

A knowledge network, which is a permanent organizational structure
with an underlying life cycle within an arranged framework, i.e. it is formally built and has clear roles and responsibilities, seemed to meet all the
criteria for such an integration architecture. It would, furthermore, provide
a space in which the network participants could transfer implicit knowledge on the level of the facilitating conditions that are analogous to an appropriate atmosphere. Such a network would also provide employees with
the opportunity to interact with one another on the level of knowledge
work processes.

A knowledge network initiative is not and should not be separated from
other functions within the company. Integration and coordination with
other functions should be aimed at consolidating the daily business and at
overcoming the functional islands within a company. Integration and coordination will enable the realization of the promised improvement in the
daily business and will clarify the advantages of a knowledge network.
However,, knowledge network members have to rely on the knowledge
and experience of the non-participants so as not to reinvent the wheel.

Our initial departure point for the research project was the existing
MERLIN methodology with its underlying reference model, which consists of facilitating conditions, knowledge processes and knowledge network architecture. All three layers of the reference model have their inter-

related step in the MERLIN methodology, which ought to be considered when setting up a knowledge network in order to gain its functionality. This approach, however, takes into account the whole life cycle of the knowledge network. Based on the time restriction of the research project and the fact that we built the knowledge network from scratch, we were only able to investigate the precondition for a knowledge network and its initial phase. The organization of the process within the network could not be observed nor could the integration of performance measurements. Since the project was carried out in close cooperation with RWE Net representatives, the companies' restrictions and indications were to be considered, e.g. an indication of the business field of street lighting and the restriction of the company's lack of a knowledge vision.

In the following sections, we want to describe, as depicted in Figure 2.2, the observed and indicated issues in order to develop an M&A integration network. In particular, we want to examine each of the three layers of the reference model and the related steps of the MERLIN methodology that are specific to the situation in RWE Net and the post-merger integration after M&A, and could be observed in the preparing and initial phases of the knowledge network [10].

Commitment of the top management and of the members, and the selection of the management board are specific to the layer of the facilitating conditions. On the layer of the knowledge processes, we look at the selection of network members, the identification of success factors and barriers, and the facilitation of building relationship within the network. On the layer of knowledge network processes, we describe the organization of the meetings and the communication between the members.

---

[10] These steps diverge from the MERLIN methodology, which describes the set up of an intra-organizational knowledge network.

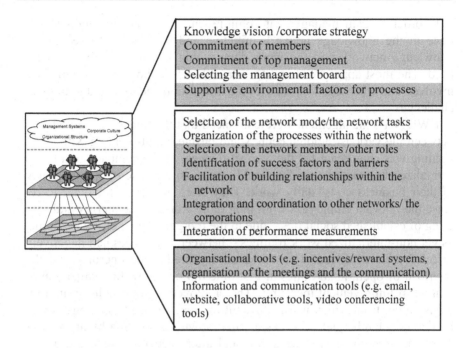

| Knowledge vision /corporate strategy |
| Commitment of members |
| Commitment of top management |
| Selecting the management board |
| Supportive environmental factors for processes |

| Selection of the network mode/the network tasks |
| Organization of the processes within the network |
| Selection of the network members /other roles |
| Identification of success factors and barriers |
| Facilitation of building relationships within the network |
| Integration and coordination to other networks/ the corporations |
| Integration of performance measurements |

| Organisational tools (e.g. incentives/reward systems, organisation of the meetings and the communication) |
| Information and communication tools (e.g. email, website, collaborative tools, video conferencing tools) |

Fig. 2.2 Steps suggested by the MERLIN Methodology

Management Commitment

Once the business need had been revealed and an appropriate organizational structure had been decided on, the setting up of a knowledge network was started. Since a knowledge network is a formally set-up structure, it implicates management acceptance and support. The commitment of the RWE Net management was therefore crucial for the knowledge network's survival, as the management had to provide the required financial, personal as well as organizational resources. Their acceptance and support of a knowledge network facilitate participants' involvement, since their participation within a knowledge network will then not be questioned but rather be appreciated (Büchel and Raub, 2002, p. 591). Management commitment plays an important role in the setting up of a knowledge network as well as during the kick-off workshop. Before the kick-off workshop, the RWE Net management released the resources, and during the kick-off workshop, management involvement underpinned the importance of the knowledge network.

In order to gain management commitment, management ought to believe in the knowledge network initiative and they ought to see that a knowledge network and the work done within it can solve the business need. The most appropriate managers are therefore those who are directly involved and who have to deal with the integration and knowledge transfer challenges.

RWE Net's management were convinced that the transfer of knowledge between the various regional centers and business units dealing with street lighting was significant for the competitiveness of the company and that a formalized knowledge transfer would ensure an increase in the efficiency of their business units' daily work. They were, however, reluctant to release the relevant employees from their daily work, as the merger and severing of established social ties – due to the reorganization, changes and the as yet non-internalized work routines – between employees had negatively affected their workload. The workload appeared to be onerous, and the overload of operational duties at that time did not allow the realization of long-term improvement measures. The employees were caught up in a vicious circle, from which it was difficult to break loose. An analogy would be that of a lumberjack who has to chop down trees with a blunt axe: the work requires much physical effort and after each felled tree the axe is blunter and the work more laborious. When he is advised to hone the axe, he replies that he has no time to do so because he has to fell as many trees as fast as possible.

As the challenges of knowledge integration and transfer only affect parts of the company, the management representatives were selected for the road shows on the strength of their involvement in the challenges of knowledge integration and transfer. These road shows, during which the many benefits of a knowledge network were presented and underpinned with examples from the unsatisfactory prevailing situation, were used to persuade the management. Additionally, an esteemed manager served as the figurehead of the project; he was convinced of the urgency of the need for a knowledge network, and was disposed to promote the idea. It was of the utmost importance that all managers believed in the knowledge network initiative.

There were two issues that the managers had to understand. Firstly, they had to recognize the urgency of the business' need. They had to realize that the business field of street lighting and the sharing of knowledge of this field are essential for the competitiveness of the company, since important contracts would be expiring within a few years. Secondly, they had to understand that in the long run a knowledge network would deliver more time for all employees, because they could benefit from the work done by the knowledge network members. However, participation in a knowledge network would require time, as the members would have to contribute work, and thus time, to the network. Managers would benefit from the knowledge network's bringing people together to find solutions in the field of street lighting, since this could lead to the performance of the regional centers being enhanced in future. While the presentation during the road shows created a belief in the demand for a knowledge network, figures contributed greatly to convincing of the management. The figures were presented in a business plan[11] that included the details of the estimated results, as well as the required financial, personal and organizational resources. The management was convinced by the fact that obtained results would mean a decrease in the expenditure.

In order to involve the management in the knowledge network, a management board, a formal group of managers whose employees would participate in and exercise control over the activities of the network, was established. They are all regional center leaders and were therefore all connected by means of regular meetings before the set up of a knowledge network. Although they accepted their role on the management board, their regular meetings mean that they do not require additional meetings for the control of the knowledge network's work. The management board provides the knowledge network with an appropriate direction. It also delivers the required resources to the knowledge network by releasing its members from other work. The management board furthermore controls the performance of the knowledge network, i.e. the knowledge network participants have to report on the work done during regular meetings with the board. The members of the management board have decision-making power, and a sufficient strategic overview of the relevant company issues. With the establishment of the management board, the knowledge network finally gained significance within the company.

Selection of Knowledge Network Participants

A knowledge network is comprised of people sharing implicit knowledge and interacting with one another. Only the appropriate composition of people ensures an effective and efficient knowledge sharing and collaboration within the knowledge network. The identification and selection of the appropriate knowledge network participants were thus crucial for its future performance. Although a knowledge network is a self-regulated structure, some, previously determined, specific roles and responsibilities, such as those of a knowledge network leader or its members, are required to guarantee focused work.

---

[11] For a detailed description of the business plan see p. 194

The participants have to be aware of a structure within a group. Although a knowledge network is, or should be, a largely self-regulated organizational form, there are roles and responsibilities within each group as well as a hierarchy. There should be no doubt who the leader is and what the participants' roles in such a group are. A group has to be well composed. The group members need to have adequate social and professional skills and similar backgrounds. This is important because they have to speak a similar language and understand one another. Since the members of the knowledge network come together not to talk, but to solve problems, the members need to have a meaningful activity. They, or the group leader, have to find a task for them.

The very first identified and selected member of the knowledge network was the network leader, since the leader plays a pivotal role. The specific merger-related barriers had indicated that certain competencies were needed. The network leader did not have to be an expert on street lighting, although he had to have an understanding of street lighting, i.e. know the challenges, the terminology, and rudimentary procedures. The knowledge leader had to be a confident person and, if possible, be previously known to the participants, which induces trust. Further selection criteria were that the leader had to be familiar with the concept of a knowledge network, and know how to deal with a divergent group. The leader would be responsible for the preparation of the first meeting and for the realization and coordination of further meetings during which the leader would coordinate and focus the members on the objectives. He had to be a "primus inter pares" (von Krogh et al., 2001b, p. 423).

The organization chart enabled the identification of potential members, since specific posts in street lighting had been perpetuated after the merger. The road shows and conducted interviews provided information on street lighting experts, as informal networks still remained.

The identification and selection of the network members were determined by the findings of the preconditions for a knowledge network. Therein, the knowledge related to the process and task of a knowledge network, as well as the knowledge gaps and overlaps within the provision of street lighting had been identified. A more qualitative selection factor relied on the employees' interest in the specific knowledge topic of street lighting and concessionary contracts. Building on this insight, the knowledge network leader provided the management board with the requirements that potential knowledge network participants had to meet and they were then duly chosen. The management involvement thus not only supported the allocation of network members, but also enhanced the identification of experts with the most appropriate knowledge pertaining to the work within the network.

Involvement of Knowledge Network Participants

The identification of the potential members for a knowledge network was merely the initial step towards the constitution of an active knowledge network. During the interviews the company's representatives indicated that potential knowledge network members might be reluctant to participate. Barriers to the establishment of a knowledge network were therefore not only encountered on the level of the managerial hierarchy, but also on that of potential knowledge network participants, the latter covering a wide field. In addition, there were organizational barriers, such as the geographical dispersion of the employees, but also personal barriers related to the merger and the subsequent integration initiatives:

- During the previous few years, RWE Energie and VEW Energie employees had experienced many changes. Their capacity to accept new initiatives was limited.
- It was found that the employees were skeptical of the new changes, which also influenced their attitude. In order to regain their confidence they needed a period of rest and a firm basis from which to approach their work.
- There were differing opinions on how the topic of the knowledge management initiative should be approached. Some people preferred a technical approach, while others preferred a more organizational approach.
- There were time constraints due to the reorganization and the subsequent workload.

These barriers had to be kept in mind during the first meeting of the participants, which thus aimed at creating mutual understanding and a mutual knowledge base. In direct contrast to the barriers, was the value to be gained from the network participation, also indicated by the interviewees. There were two value groups affecting each potential member's personal motivation.

- Personal value: The employees could enhance their reputations by participating in a knowledge network, because they would be regarded as experts by their co-workers. The expert status that the participants would enjoy within their working environment represents a strategic value in that they would be difficult to replace. Their participation would lead to facilitation of their work, as they would have contact with other experts who could help them solve problems quickly. Finally, participation would provide an "escape" from daily business and enable the forming of valuable social ties.

- Value for the business unit: Participation in a knowledge network would lead to the newest knowledge on street lighting being shared by all the participants, which would lead to the general improvement of the issue in focus.

These values to be gained were used, on the one hand, in the business plan; especially the value for the business unit while the strategic value provided a significant breakthrough in management commitment. On the other hand, the personal value was used as a stimulation to encourage participants to attend the first meeting as well as providing a mutual understanding of the participants' motives for participating. In fact, the interviewees emphasized the personal value as a crucial issue in the establishment of the knowledge network. The employees from one of the original companies were familiar with another type of organizational form resembling knowledge networks, i.e. working groups. However, the working groups were regarded as non-effective and time consuming.

To prevent the knowledge network from being regarded in the same light, its work had to be linked to short-term and long-term objectives from the beginning. This was also in line with the management intention and the business need, as the interviewees revealed. The best short- and long-term results, however, are achieved by a knowledge network initiative if its task is derived from the business goals of company growth, such as to gain new customers and provide new services to old customers. Continuous alignment with these goals guarantees that the participants' work is clearly focused and facilitates management commitment.

The short-term objectives would demonstrate the efficiency of the knowledge network to the managers and participants. The short-term objectives could be met if the participants of the knowledge network concentrated on the transfer of documents and approaches used at RWE Energie and VEW Energie, and if they got to know their fellow participants' abilities. The long-term objectives would convey the development of the employees' knowledge. They would focus on problem solving and generating new knowledge. Since the affiliation to the knowledge network is task related, the objective of the task to be solved is twofold. Firstly, the task should aim at the harmonization of contractual proceedings, and should therefore increase RWE Net's competitive position. Secondly, the task to be solved by the former RWE Energie and VEW Energie employees should be aimed at reducing prejudices and at removing the barriers between them.

Establishment of Social Ties

The first meeting of the participants plays a significant role in the further progress of the knowledge network, since the participants have to cope with a new situation and with a new form of working. They need a stimulus to overcome the inertia of their daily business. A discussion on what motivates and what might hinder the members from participating in the network should clarify the triggers and barriers. Since the geographical dispersion of the knowledge network members entails a virtual cooperation, initializing trust is a major effort. Research has shown that establishment of mutual understanding and trust building are facilitated by candid initial communication (Jarvenpaa and Leidner, 1999, p. 806 ff.). The participants of a knowledge network can create social ties during initial face-to-face meetings. Knowledge sharing especially requires mutual understanding and trust (von Krogh et al., 2001b).

Initial barriers, however, can appear during the first meeting and the first phase of a knowledge network's life cycle. They generally take the form of a lack of member commitment to the group, due to a lack of trust, unclear roles, misunderstandings, or acting as individual actors within the group (Wenger et al., 2002, p. 71 ff.). These barriers affect the performance of the group in the first phase. At RWE Net, too, initial barriers to its knowledge network had to be overcome in order to create group coherence. This is usually an extensive process, but to accelerate it at RWE Net a two-day kick-off workshop was organized, during which the participants revealed their interest in joining the group and got to know one another. Since they had been chosen by their superiors, they could not really refuse to attend. Therefore the external motivational aspects, i.e. management direction, were strong enough to overcome barriers to joining the kick-off workshop.

The participants had been involved in several integration projects for at least two years, all had dealt with the area of street lighting and they formed a cross-functional and cross-geographical group. They came from different regional centers, different business units, had different professional backgrounds, and the group consisted equally of former VEW Energie and RWE Energie employees.

The first meeting of the knowledge network members is described in accordance with the team-developing circle (cf. Tuckman, 1965). It compromises four stages, the first step is the phase of carefully checking one another, since they ought to recognize their position in the group and the other participants. Once they have recognized their position in the group, the phase of fighting begins, e.g. dominant persons want to establish their leading position. In order to create an effective group, the norming phase has to be established through a common agreement between the participants, which would lead to the phase of performing, in which the participants create a committed group.

The first day served as a warming up, it was the phase of carefully checking one another and gaining insights into the knowledge network initiative. At the beginning of the first day, the participants created personal information posters on which their names, their working experiences, the affiliation to RWE Net and private activities were recorded. After an introduction by a manager that emphasized the management's interest in this project, the network leader gave a presentation on the concept of knowledge management and knowledge networks. During the presentation he emphasized the urgency of the matter and the value that the company would gain from a formal transfer of knowledge of street lighting between the regional centers and across business units. The first day ended with a dinner that provided time to socialize and get to know one another as individuals.

The second day of the kick-off workshop was held at a different location, namely on a small island, and with no management representatives present. The company uses the location for exclusive events only, and it was thus an honor to be invited, emphasizing the strategic importance of the network initiative. The absence of management representatives would also create openness among the participants and lead them to trust one another. The island itself was analogous to all participants sitting in the same boat, being an entity, and needing to solve the task jointly. During this day, the other three phases of the team-developing circle started appearing.

The phase of fighting began when the participants had to list the unsolved challenges of the post-merger integration. They could not agree on the unsolved challenges. Some even had difficulties identifying any topic or problem, as they were under the impression that they were there to solve problems not find them. Hidden conflicts were revealed as well as the fact that other project teams were already working on the same problems. The representatives of the project team, and especially their leaders, feared losing their power; they possessed a knowledge asset, and wanted to remain an exclusive group. The proposed network would also disturb hidden agendas. The disagreements immediately made the heterogeneous nature of the group visible in that most of the participants were already involved in newly formed project teams, while the information regarding the already undertaken initiatives was news for other participants.

In an effort to pacify the proceedings, the leader listed the various existing project groups dealing with street lighting; their names, goals, topics, members, and noting the type of documentation in which the newly generated knowledge was captured. Each participant then described the street lighting topic on which he or she was working. The description of street lighting projects revealed their knowledge, which led to self-esteem as an accepted expert and created value in that they began to know one another. These activities organized and aligned the group, which is the third stage of the team developing circle and a precondition for the next and last stage.

The knowledge network leader subsequently identified the existing blind spots in the field of street lighting and the personal benefits that each participant would receive by working on such a topic. By doing so she drew attention to tasks that needed to be done to reach the planned strategic value and depicted the need for a formal organizational form like a knowledge network.

The fourth phase of the team-developing circle, i.e. the phase of integration, could be observed as the blind spots were described. The descriptions of the blind spots enhanced each participant's understanding of his or her situation as well as that of the challenges faced by the other participants'. All the participants became aware that some topics were still not being covered, and that there was no flow of collected information on street lighting between the business units, or between the project teams and the rest of the organization. These blind spots would form the activities of the knowledge network. Each of the blind spots was described under three headings, so that the participants could analyze the gaps.

The first heading included the name of the blind spots and a short description, the second heading depicted the tasks to be done, i.e. formal vs. informal tasks or standardized tasks, and the third heading covered the objective of the tasks and the related work procedures. The whole self-deciding and revealing process increased the group's commitment, regardless of whether they wanted to form a network or not, and clarified the consequence of the participation, e.g. tasks, and values, for those who chose the network option. This communal and open way of decision making created a group dynamic, which furthermore illustrated the disadvantage of not participating if a network were to be setup.

Further Development of the Knowledge Network

After the kick-off workshop, a communication plan was drawn up, according to which the obtained workshop results were documented and sent to the participants for their perusal. The communication plan had two aims. Firstly, the documentation of the knowledge network activities had to be presented to the managers, since they exercised control over the knowledge network and wanted to see tangible outcomes. Secondly, the communication plan contained the initial and further proceedings of the knowledge network. It detailed the roles and responsibilities of the knowledge network participants, their knowledge related to the business field of street lighting as well as what the subsequent activities of the participants would be, including milestones. The participants' agreement with the results and future activities of a knowledge network is the basis for trouble-free cooperation in the succeeding phases of the knowledge network life cycle. After the participants had corroborated the content, the results were sent to the management board.

The kick-off workshop is the start of the knowledge network. The subsequent face-to-face meetings build on the gained results of the kick-off workshop. Although the task to be solved by the knowledge network members and the purpose of the knowledge network were related to the company's strategy and its daily business, it was possible that their involvement with their normal business unit tasks could eventually absorb all their energy and time. In order for the members of the knowledge network to retain momentum, a pattern of regular meetings has to be established (Nahapiet and Ghoshal, 1998, p. 251 ff.). The rhythm of the meetings delivers the required familiarity with the network and has a positive impact on trust building, and, ultimately, on the integration of the employees. Additionally, the regularity of the meetings guarantees that the visibility of the knowledge network will be maintained

Since the participants' daily workload is high and the tasks of the network ought to be solved in time, their cooperation should result in frequent communication, but not specifically in face-to-face meetings. The physical distances, however, between the participants might make difficult to maintain the interaction and communication (Govindarajan and Gupta, 2001). One way of overcoming the lack of direct interaction and face-to-face communication within the knowledge network is through the use of ICT tools. They comprise the full range between traditional communication means, such as the telephone, and the communication and document sharing means provided by new technologies, e.g., live conferencing, web casting, application sharing and team spaces. The ICT tools required by members of RWE Net's knowledge networks depend on the life cycle of their specific network (Raimann, 2002, p. 179).

At first, the currently available infrastructure such as e-mail, a common folder on a central server or telephone, is used, since the needs of the knowledge networks members tend to be simple. In other words, any technology that enables communication and places to meet and talk will do. Later, an ICT tool that supports knowledge management and allows the members to post questions or supply answers, to share documents, and coordinate their work ought to be considered (Gongla and Rizzuto, 2001). The network leader has to take into account that the use of these tools depends on the richness of the content and the tools' frequency of use. For instance, a low utilization rate of ICT tools, especially the asynchronous communication, might give the impression that the knowledge network is dead. To avoid this, a threaded discussion is useful, i.e. the knowledge network leader stimulates communication by posting a message or question, or the leader sends an e-mail mentioning the newest issues and includes a link to a corresponding folder.

As the knowledge network proceeds and the members are about to achieve the first outcomes, the knowledge network can be made more visible within the company. The increased visibility is achieved through, e.g., internal newspapers, and a web site on the intranet. This publicity popularizes the work of the members, the outcomes of the network and the knowledge network initiative. The popularization also provides the knowledge network members with a good reputation and recognition and, simultaneously, enhances the general commitment to a knowledge network.

Supporting the Performance of a Knowledge Network

The knowledge transfer activities are carried out in the face-to-face or virtual meetings. Because participation in the knowledge network aims at achieving personal value objectives that cannot be achieved by an individual, the meetings need to be well prepared in order to be useful for the members and provide the company with strategic value. They need to be aligned with the members' experience, needs, and culture, therefore a group with a similar professional background provides better results than a heterogeneous group. Since the employees come from different organizational backgrounds, it is important that the meetings take place where the members have the freedom to candidly ask advice, share their opinions, or exchange ideas that have not been fully thought through, i.e. a neutral place.

The meetings are thus aimed at providing opportunities for the sharing of explicit and, especially, tacit knowledge among the members, and at overcoming the existent barriers between the employees.

To meet the above goals and to close the knowledge gaps, the succeeding meetings ought to build on the agreed division into short- and long-term objectives as established during the kick-off workshop. The meetings should also include a discussion of the tasks to be solved during the next meeting in order to ensure the continuity of the work. The specific situation in the company entails that if these meetings are to be focused on results and efficiency, the knowledge network leader needs to ensure that the objectives to be achieved are given a project structure. This includes an agreement on individual tasks, and the determining of responsibilities and deadlines. The leader ought to see to it that the deadlines are kept. Furthermore, all activities performed and issues discussed in the network have to be documented, but they ought not to be published beyond the knowledge network.

In general, people have to realize that there is a personal value to be gained by participating in a network.

Lessons Learned

The research project revealed that despite a well-carried out analysis of the current situation and the identified and communicated business need for a formal knowledge transfer, the people involved resisted new and unfamiliar initiatives. Hidden agendas, political and power issues can also disturb new initiatives.

Despite the road show on the first day of the kick-off workshop, some participants had problems with the concepts and understanding of the terms and definitions used. Their understanding of knowledge management often also deviated from the regular understanding. They associated the organizational structure of knowledge networks, and especially its objectives, with the aims of project that already existed.

Many of the participants in the kick-off workshop and, especially, the leaders of the existing projects feared losing their power, because a network would build an additional and wider knowledge base on street lighting than they could create themselves or within their individual projects. However, the lack of comprehensive knowledge regarding existing projects revealed that a formal knowledge transfer would facilitate the work of all the involved participants. In this specific case, and quite unexpectedly, the network initiative destroyed hidden power structures by creating openness and by providing a structure without an unequal distribution of power. After the kick-off workshop, the participants appreciated the fact that they had gained an overview of those projects in the pipeline or being implemented at that time.

A successful group work is based on three necessary, but not sufficient, structural conditions. The three conditions are: 1) a clear and explicit determination of roles and responsibilities, 2) a well composed group with adequate social and professional skills with similar backgrounds, and 3) meaningful activity (Hackman, 1990). It appeared that the three structural conditions for successful group work have to be established as soon as possible during the first meeting. This is especially the case when the group consists of cross-functional participants and some participants considered their knowledge a private and strategic commodity. If these conditions are not established, they may inhibit the subsequent proceedings of the knowledge network.

A mutual understanding of the concepts used as well as of the other participants' experience and the business challenges, provides the opportunity for subsequent interaction and communication in the knowledge network. The collecting of participants' expertise during the kick-off workshop formed the first step towards mutual recognition as well as towards an electronic yellow pages, and, more importantly, towards trust and openness. The collecting of the expertise provided an overview of the knowledge residing at the different regional centers and business units and enhanced the transfer of knowledge.

Usually the participants of a kick-off workshop are asked to provide an indication of unsolved challenges within their field of expertise, but with these participants this proved to be an incorrect action. It provided an opening for people with hidden agendas who did not want lose their position of power. They therefore stated that they did not know of any such challenges or said that those challenges that were mentioned, had already been solved or were being attended to in other projects.

Additionally, hierarchical thinking employees in a company with clear roles and responsibilities may actually have problems in defining tasks, which is also indicative of the management's confidence in the employees' competence, or the employees may not be ready for such responsibility as yet. Therefore, clear indications, i.e. these are the goals that are to be achieved within such a period, could be more appropriate. Nevertheless, the confrontation with the hidden agendas may still have appeared at a later date, since a confrontation was inevitable.

General Recommendations

Each company and each post-merger integration are unique. Therefore the establishment of a knowledge network aimed at integrating the employees' knowledge and contributing to the growth of a company needs to be adapted. The following general recommendations have been derived as the most important issues for the establishing and maintaining of a knowledge network. The derivation of the general recommendations results from discussions and generalizations during workshops with knowledge managers from multinational companies facing similar situations. They follow the above-described case's line of reasoning.

- The knowledge network initiative gains its full impact when it follows the technical and organizational integration of a company. The results of the earlier phases of the integration can be used to set up the knowledge network. Integration managers should also be involved in the setting up of a knowledge network, because their experience during the earlier integration efforts can be useful.
- The management should be involved in the knowledge network initiative as soon as possible. If they are not the initiators of the knowledge network, they should be the providers of resources and of facilitating conditions.
- Due to the specific situation of a merger and the related barriers, such as the fear of losing jobs and unwillingness to deal with unknown organizational forms, a "list of benefits", i.e. qualitative outcomes, is needed to convince the management and the prospective members of the value of sharing tacit knowledge through a knowledge network.
- The identification of the knowledge gaps within the company is significant for the further progress of the knowledge network. The task to be solved by the members, derived from the knowledge gaps, has to be knowledge intensive, i.e. it not only requires explicit knowledge, but also cooperation by the members. It is crucial to have a business need that is directly linked to an important strategic value for the company and linked directly to company's growth aims.
- Still existing (informal) networks in both previous organizations can help to identify appropriate members for as well as helping to build the new knowledge network.
- People constitute a knowledge network, therefore they should initiate it. They have to see the need to eliminate knowledge and integration gaps in their daily business. When they realize that their managers appreciate their initiative, and that the benefits from participation in the knowledge network outweigh the drawbacks, merger-related barriers will no longer be significant.
- Although ICT tools provide the means with which to communicate and interact with other people, social ties are best established when the knowledge network participants meet face-to-face, which helps to create trust and openness. This is especially true if the participants come from different pre-merger or acquired companies, since different notions and different approaches have to be aligned. The first meeting has to be used to create a shared understanding of the concepts used in the succeeding activities. The knowledge network participants ought to identify their common interests as well. This facilitates the identification with one another.

- Since a knowledge network functions parallel with the business structure, regular meetings, whether virtual or face-to-face, generate the needed stability for the knowledge network's activities and strengthens the social ties. Communication of the achieved results to the management board should only be done with the knowledge network participants' agreement.
- In keeping with the aims of the tasks to be achieved, the formal organization of meetings provides the management and members with value. Outcome-oriented meetings with a standardized agenda enable value creation. In order to propagate the outcomes generated in a knowledge network, work done in it has to be linked to the integration approaches within the company. Participants can share their knowledge in their daily business while the management board can pick up the knowledge and share it in their daily environment as well as doing internal marketing for the knowledge network activities.

3 The Customer – an Untapped Source of Innovation. Developing a Customer Integration Network in HP

Grzegorz Gurgul[1], Ellen Enkel[1], Maria Rumyantseva[1] and Claudia Ulrich[2]

[1]Research Center KnowledgeSource, University of St. Gallen, Switzerland
[2]Representative of HP Support Center, Germany

Abstract

In general, a company has to overcome two environmental challenges. First of all, customers drive a company's business through their demands and their preferences. They can demand much from a company, since changing to another vendor is quite easy in a buyer's market. Secondly, technology-intensive companies face a swiftly changing competitive environment characterized by shortened product and service life cycles as well as by knowledge-dependent products and services.

In order to overcome these challenges and ensure organic growth, a company should launch customer-required product and services and become more customer centered, thus increasing customer loyalty. And this requires a better understanding of customers. It therefore follows that customers' requirements can be better fulfilled by directly involving them in the innovation process.

The main purpose of the bilateral project between the HP support and the researchers of KnowledgeSource was thus to develop a model that would support the integration of both explicit and implicit customer knowledge, i.e. it would enable constant bilateral knowledge flows between the customers and the company in order to improve products and services.

HP's historical background is described, followed by the internal and external challenges that the company faces. Thereafter the approach to the suggested solution – the steps leading to the building of a knowledge network – is described. The case is concluded with the most important lessons learned and general recommendations.

Customer Involvement in Internal Processes

Conceptual Background

Product and service innovations are the key drivers of a company's growth. Innovation generation, however, is a highly creative, knowledge intensive, and, sometimes, a difficult to manage process. Only a small part of the ideas at the beginning of the innovation process will eventually become competitive products and services (Tschirky and Koruna, 1998).

Innovation generation can be approached via two methods: it can be either market driven or technology driven. Technology-driven innovations are an inside-out approach, i.e. the company generates a new technology, product or service and introduces it to the market. Market-driven innovation is characterized by cognizance being taken of the market and, especially, customers' peculiarities (Kodama, 1995).

From the point of view of product and service innovation, a technology intensive company is confronted with environmental and internal issues. Environmental issues lead to shortened product life cycles, which requires swifter knowledge transfer and application within a company in order to generate innovations, i.e. new products and services (Kenney, 2001; North, 1999). The value of products and services, however, depends more on knowledge factors, such as technological know-how, understanding of the customers and service competency, and less on material resources (Picot et al., 2001; Pierer, 2000).

Consequently, a company needs to build a knowledge base as quickly as possible and permanently augment and alter it in order to acquire and maintain its knowledge requirements. Innovations are not an end in themselves, but the better they anticipate customer requirements, the better products and services are accepted by customers, which entails a higher loyalty.

Without an understanding of the different types of customer requirements, a company risks providing superfluous quality, driving customers to competitors or focusing only on what the customer says, and not on what the customer thinks (Kano, 1984). Customer requirements can be further divided into two dimensions, i.e. degree of fulfillment and customer satisfaction.

Three types of customer requirements can be identified: expected, normal and latent requirements. The expected requirements are so obvious that the customer does not even notice them when they are present, e.g. an airbag in a new car. They do not provide any competitive advantage, therefore it would be waste of a company's time to identify these requirements. Normal requirements, however, are required and articulated by customers, e.g., the price and performance of a product. A company has to take into account that if these needs are met, the customer is satisfied, if not, the customer is dissatisfied and might change to another provider. Latent requirements are not consciously needed and if a company does not meet these requirements, customers do not complain. Nevertheless, if a company understands such needs and fulfills them, the customer is highly satisfied and such products or services will be successful and will probably provide a higher competitive advantage, e.g., Sony's Walkman and 3M's Post-it®.

Besides this static view of customers' requirements, there is also a dynamic view of that states that after a while normal requirements become expected requirements and the latent requirements, once detected by a company, are going to be imitated by other competitors and will then become normal requirements. For instance, an airbag expressed a latent requirement to be protected from accidents, nowadays an airbag is normal and even an expected requirement. Consequently, a company that wants to stay competitive and customer oriented should continuously anticipate and adapt to environmental changes and challenges and customers' needs.

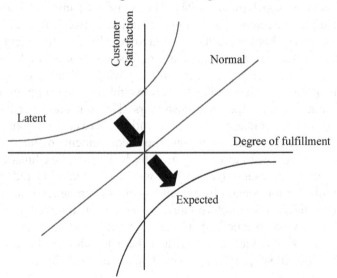

Fig. 3.1 Three types of requirements and its dynamic view (Source: Kano, 1984)

Companies can anticipate customer demands through market mechanism, such as transaction tracking and surveys. This type of anticipation of customer demand is built on a one-way flow of knowledge with companies collecting explicit knowledge from the customer. Conversely, however, leading-edge customers have gained experience and knowledge of companies' products and services, which can contribute to the improvement of products and services and to innovations that could even fulfill latent customer requirements (von Hippel, 1988).

By working closely with its customer Intel, Shinko, a Japanese semiconductor-packaging manufacturer, was able to meet Intel's packaging design requirements for various chip forms, and became a key supplier. Such knowledge is embedded within customers as implicit knowledge, i.e. knowledge to be obtained from customers, which is sometimes more pivotal for the anticipation of customer needs than knowledge about customers (Garcia-Murillo and Annabi, 2002). Nevertheless, companies often neglect knowledge to be obtained from customer, since the one-way flow of knowledge needs to be altered into a bi-directional flow of knowledge (Davenport et al., 2001; Garcia-Murillo and Annabi, 2002).

The establishment of a bi-directional knowledge flow and thus meeting even latent customer requirements necessitates a different approach than mere attention to market mechanisms. The transfer and integration of implicit knowledge are, however, more demanding than the transfer of explicit knowledge (von Hippel, 1994). The transfer of implicit knowledge requires a direct interaction and communication between the sender and the receiver, since this knowledge is sometimes difficult to articulate and the sender is often not aware that he possesses this kind of knowledge (Polanyi, 1966). Consequently, if a company wants to meet the latent requirements of its customers, it has to gain insight into their implicit knowledge, i.e. obtain knowledge from customers. This, on the other hand, requires a direct interaction and cooperation between customers and company to allow customers to express their requirements better.

An organizational structure, supported by ICT tools, that links customers and company representatives and allows direct interaction and communication could be the means by which to transfer embedded knowledge. Such an organizational structure can be found in a knowledge network. Besides the above-mentioned advantages, a knowledge network that integrates customers' knowledge would also help to address the challenges faced within the HP support in Germany that are described next.

The Company Background

In 1938, Hewlett Packard's first product – a resistance capacity radio oscillator – was launched. Walt Disney ordered eight oscillators for the production of Fantasia. One year later William R. Hewlett and David Packard, both graduates of Stanford University, founded the company. Their first headquarters was in a small garage in Palo Alto, California, making these entrepreneurs two of the founders of Silicon Valley. Since then, HP has invented and launched new technologies and products and maintained its position as a leading and innovative enterprise. Among many exceptional technologies, the company developed a high-speed frequency counter in the '50s, in the '60s the world's first scientific desktop calculator and in the '70s the world's first, and most famous, hand-held scientific calculator.

HP does not only have a leading position in the field of new technologies, or innovative products, but also in reinventing itself as an organization. The firm has been introducing innovative management methods for the last 60 years. In the 1940s David Packard created the concept of "Management by Walking Around", during the same period HP established the "Open Door Policy", and in the 1960s it was among the first companies in the world to introduce flexible working hours.

Today HP is one of the leading computer and IT companies and has sales and support offices located in 160 countries worldwide. Its headquarters is still in Palo Alto, California. The product range includes: desktops and workstations, mobile products, printing and digital imaging equipment, storage equipment, servers, as well as software for HP hardware – this diversity guarantees it the leading position in the field of information services.

HP's Way to Customer Involvement

As a technology-intensive company, HP cannot afford to lose its technological leadership. Thus HP's core paradigm – and major path to growth – is innovation. Innovation is also incorporated into HP's vision (see HP's vision p. 103). The company concentrates on both the technology-driven as well on the market-driven approach to innovation. The market-driven approach is based on learning from customers and their interaction with HP, which entails openness to customers' ideas and insights. This is a shift from a product-centered to a customer-oriented approach. The significance of moving towards being a customer-oriented organization is twofold. Firstly, HP can gain more knowledge from the customer in order to anticipate customer demands. Secondly, the anticipation may increase HP's customer loyalty, since keeping customers is easier than gaining new customers (Sviokla and Shapiro, 1993).

On its way towards being a customer-oriented organization, HP launched the Total Customer Experience (TCE) program. The business customer with his problems and insights into products and ideas is the primary focus of this program. The overall objective of the program is to ameliorate customer support and learn from customers during the entire customer life cycle[12]. On the one hand, the purpose of the TCE program is to support the processes that remove internal company barriers to knowledge exchange as well as to support those processes that create customer solutions. On the other hand, the purpose of the TCE program is to provide customers with a good impression of HP as based on their experience with its products, services, solutions, and people.

As HP's history has revealed, HP is an agile enterprise that is able to re-invent itself. Despite the strategic importance of innovation for the company and the focus on customers, a formalized customer network was a new and unknown phenomenon. HP's employees were, nevertheless, appreciative of customer input and aware of the knowledge their customers harbored, this insight being based on the company's thorough TCE program. This program is deeply anchored in the employees' routines, since the TCE program definitely influences their work, especially that of employees who are in direct contact with customers.

Although customer centricity is a challenge that the company as a whole has to work towards, the case wants to describe the issues in the service department [13]. The support center, through its direct interface with customers, was specifically confronted with this challenge. The service department has to provide solutions to customer problems, and consequently also receives feedback on products and services. Ensuring an optimal smooth workflow for customers would thus entail integrating and aligning customer processes into HP's process world.

Customers expect consistent and seamless support across product categories, which requires close collaboration among HP's various support business divisions. The support center wanted to save financial resources and optimize personal cognitive resources within HP as well as in the customers' company by speeding up the problem solving process and minimizing the interruption of the systems used. HP, in fact, needed to know

---

[12] The life cycle is divided into four steps: the customer is aware of HP's products and services, selects and purchases these product or service, thereafter gains initial experiences with them, and, finally, re-purchases them.

[13] Hewlett-Packard GmbH represents the business interests in Germany. They employ more than 5'000 people and focus on the customer support.

about the customer's problem even before it occurred. It was therefore essential that the support center got to know its customers better and facilitated the feedback and knowledge flow. Thus, the knowledge flow between the HP support and the customers had to be systematized and stabilized in order to establish a real cooperation besides receiving information from the customers.

The Demand for a Customer Knowledge Network

The usual ways of communication and interaction are characterized by time pressure and a certain kind of anonymity. A telephone call has to be executed as fast as possible, since it is a sign of good service performance, and the services' web-pages, where customers can find the solution to their problems and post questions, are the two major means of communication and interaction. Needless to say, these ways of interaction do not lead to a learning situation that needs time and personal contact.

The HP support wanted to learn how to become a better customer-centered company from its customers, because it recognized that there was a knowledge gap between the launched services and the customers' need for support. For example, an HP support employee who works on site at a customer company is expected to exactly understand what support is required. This deeper understanding of customers' needs could not be gained by the support staff's usual way of communication and interaction.

Over the years the support center has established good relationships with its customers, with some business customers being brought together in a community called the Bonner Group. Customers and support center representatives met in this group in order to share their opinions about the services and possible problems concerning the service. The relationships within this group were, however, only loosely linked and informal and could not lead to the formalization of knowledge transfer and the creation of long-lasting relations, since this types of relationship does not allow knowledge creation to occur (Kodama, 2002).

Challenges Faced by the HP Support Center

In order to allow customers to proffer their experiences regarding HP's products and services as well as to learn from them, HP's support wanted to establish an organizational structure that would provide an opportunity for bi-directional knowledge flow. This formalization of the transfer of knowledge and the constitution of a knowledge network were not all plain sailing. First the company had to ask itself if the support center could actually admit to the customers that it needed help from them. Additionally, financial, mental, and cognitive resources from the support center as well as from customers' companies were needed for a formalized organizational structure.

The major challenges relate to the external resources, i.e. provided by the customers. Their primary resource is the cognitive one. The customers' cognitive resources were they themselves, they had to reveal what they know. Although all customers are valuable for a company, an organizational structure enabling knowledge transfer only requires the selection of relevant customers, since not all of them can be included and not all customers have the required knowledge. A company can identify leading-edge customers by listening carefully to their comments, since appropriate customers have their own ideas and desires and express constructive opinions concerning the company's services and products, although their critical opinions might astound the company. Nonetheless, these are the customers who could deliver the insights needed to improve customer support and product improvements.

The participants are required to have a common language and to understand one another in order to interact and communicate better. Shared understanding and a common language can not be guaranteed, not even when people are physically close, and are observing and discussing the same environment. However, appropriate participant selection, a shared environment and the opportunity to talk together do facilitate these issues.

The customers, however, do not need to, nor can they be forced to, work with the company and they need their management's permission to join a formalized organizational structure. Thus HP had to convince their managements to provide permission by communicating the value that their companies would gain by joining the knowledge network. It is important that the initiator company creates a situation in which the customers can gain more from participation than from remaining outside the closer relationship. Consequently, even before the initial starting point of a formalized organizational structure, the values that the participants can expect should be clarified. In turn, this will act as a motivation for participation.

However, permission to join a formalized organizational structure does not automatically induce knowledge sharing. Customers and the company have to be willing to open their knowledge bases to each other, since participating passively and not delivering valuable insights would be a waste of resources. Only if customers are motivated, they will share their valuable knowledge and can HP reach its proposed goals. The question of how the members of a customer company can be motivated to share their knowledge should be urgently addressed.

Within the support center a further question was raised concerning the power that the network needed to have. The power to use resources and create new products and services should be addressed by each company individually, although this can lead to a better knowledge network performance. It is sensible to remember that limited power could decrease the members' motivation and minimize the value of the network, since the work done could not be realized.

The performance of a learning situation depends on efficient interaction and communication, which ensures the transfer of implicit knowledge. For this purpose face-to-face meetings are the evident means (Kodama, 2002). However, face-to-face meetings have to be well prepared in order to deliver the highest possible value. Furthermore, to maintain social ties between participants, the regularity with which meetings should occur has to be established. And since the participants are widely dispersed, ICT tools should provide the means to overcome the time and spatial barriers.

Knowledge sharing between customers and the company requires a regular face-to-face meeting, since a customer network that crosses company borders delivers the means by which implicit customer knowledge can be transferred to the company. An inter-organizational network inevitably entails confrontation with different cultures, different mentalities, and different languages. These differences might hinder smooth cooperation within a knowledge network, thus mutual commitment by both employees and customers is also compulsory.

Furthermore, connections made through face-to-face meetings form the foundation of an individual's acceptance as part of a group (Nahapiet and Ghoshal, 1998). If a knowledge network's starting point is based on a face-to-face meeting, this especially enhances the group membership. During this first meeting the participants may recognize that they belong within the network and get to know the other participants.

Solving tasks in conjunction with customers raises the issue of intellectual property rights as the customers usually deliver a contribution to the improvement of the service. There are various ways of approaching the management of intellectual property rights. One method is for the intellectual property rights to remain within the network, and the rights to the intellectual capital to be divided in direct proportion to the relevant person's responsibilities within the network. The more severe option is that the intellectual property rights are solely HP's possession. Needless to say, claims to intellectual property right can negatively influence the work within the knowledge network.

Intellectual property rights are also linked to the structure of the customer network. This issue is an important factor for the further work of the network. The customer network's structure can either be a hub type, or a network type. A hub structure seems to benefit only the central company, since all knowledge is centrally stored and not distributed. The most effective structure, comparable to those of open source projects, is when the company is only a knot in the network, and each member may cooperate and exchange knowledge with other members. A company should therefore establish an actual network structure through social events during which the involved participants can establish closer social ties.

A further issue concerns the link to other customers if knowledge is restricted to the network, and is only internally communicated. In such a case, the network participants have a competitive advantage, which can maintain and stabilize the customer network. Nevertheless, this also means the company can only partially benefit from the potential of the knowledge within the network, since the company can not use the outcomes for its others customers. The work done in such a network should not be solely utilized within the closed group, since one of the reasons for a customer knowledge network is for it to serve as a wider learning opportunity (Kodama, 2002).

The Approach of the Research Project

Faced with the above-mentioned challenges, the question was how the HP support center could establish an organizational structure that would ensure a bi-directional flow of knowledge between the company and its customers and would ensure a learning situation?

The HP support organization approached the KnowledgeSource team to provide insights into the formalized organizational structure called a knowledge network that would ensure the transfer of knowledge between persons, groups or even companies. In order to ensure that the outcome would be useful for all person involved, the research project was carried out by the research center representatives of KnowledgeSource at the University of St. Gallen, in close cooperation with the HP support.

Based on the existing MERLIN methodology, developed for intra-organizational knowledge network, we developed a new framework, a customer knowledge network, for a knowledge network that crosses company's boundaries and involves customers. The generation of the new framework was based on a theory study. We adapted the new framework for the needs of the HP support and its customers. The adaptation was carried out in a field study, during which we conducted semi-structured interviews with eleven HP support center representatives and five customers who were potential members of the knowledge network. The selection of the company representatives was based on their contact with customers and what they had learned from customer as well as their knowledge about which of the customers could potentially be a knowledge network member. Participant observation was carried out during the kick-off workshop, which was the initial starting point of the knowledge network, late in 2001.

Addressing the Challenges of a Customer Knowledge Network

Overcoming Companies' Internal Challenges

The objectives of the customers' integration were clear: it had to deliver a learning situation that would reveal the customers' latent and normal requirements so that the support center could provide its customers with the best service. The HP support was responsible for the customer knowledge network set-up. The knowledge network leader was the first role that was assigned within the customer knowledge network. He had an understanding of knowledge management and knowledge networks as well as of customers' problems that is required of a network leader. He was responsible for the selection of the potential members of the customer knowledge network and also had to persuade the management to deliver the required resources.

The objective of a customer knowledge network and with the HP support center as the initiator, narrowed the company members down to HP representatives who had direct contact with the customers, i.e. sales representatives, support representatives and HP outsourcing representatives. Based on these insights, the knowledge network leader found and persuaded three HP representatives to become members through his personal contact. These representatives were conscious of the value of the customers' insight and appreciated their contribution. A business plan, which included the estimated costs and benefits of a knowledge network initialization, was used to overcome the hurdle of management's commitment, since the presented figures prepared the way for such an organizational structure.

Most of the resources came from the support representatives and the power that the knowledge network would exercise was in the hands of the support representatives as well, therefore all knowledge derived from the work with the customers would remain in hands of these representatives. The management took a similar decision regarding the intellectual property rights – the customers could not claim any rights. The customers' insights

were appreciated within the support center, but the management representatives did not want to pay the customers for their contribution.

The knowledge network leader and the three representatives represented
the members of the HP support center. The structure of the customer
knowledge network was not complete, since more potential customers with
the required knowledge and motivated to join the knowledge network had
to be identified and integrated into the customer knowledge network. The
partners, that may be universities or other non-profit organization, were
covered by the research center.

The identification of potential network members from the HP support
center's list of customers was eased by interviewing customers, all of
whom which were IT specialist in their companies. The support center as
well as the interviewed customers had emphasized technical skills as a prerequisite for smooth communication and interaction, since they wanted
people who understood their problems and spoke the same (technical) language.

Besides the required knowledge the customers ought to posses, the HP
support center representatives ensured that the customers were not direct
competitors. The customers could therefore talk more freely about their latent requirements and provide insights without being afraid of losing their
competitive advantage. This implied absolute trust between the participants.

Delivering Facilitating Conditions

The establishment of trust, however, requires an extended period of time.
In the case of the HP support center, the trust building process was established through a constructive dialogue and the disclosure of the objectives
of the knowledge network. The customers from the Bonner Group trusted
the support center representatives to use their knowledge to improve the
services and products that were inconveniencing HP's customers and were
therefore willing to share these insights with the company.

Nonetheless, altruism is not customers' key driver for participating in a
network, and this was confirmed by some customers during the interviews.
They expected to receive tangible values from HP. The unifying common
point was that both sides needed to solve problems faster and more efficiently, which was also mentioned in the interviews. A common task provides a basis for smooth co-operation between the heterogeneous members
of a customer knowledge network. It was thus vital to establish a link between the motivation and the task. A feasible link was that the invited cus-

tomers could choose from a sample of possible tasks that had been identified by both company representatives and customers during the interviews.

The members of a customer network should experience the benefits of their participation as quickly as possible – the longer it takes to achieve tangible results, the more important financial incentives become. The first task to be solved should always be low hanging fruit, i.e. the concretization of expected requirements in the services provided as well as their improvement. In the HP case, for instance, customer data management, which includes collaboration and the exchange of information between the customers and the HP support center, was identified as an expected requirement.

Initializing the Customer Knowledge Network

The concept of a customer knowledge network and its tasks should be explained to the customers and a face-to-face meeting is the most efficient way to communicate these issues. This meeting takes the form of a kick-off workshop aimed at creating trust and making the tangible objectives of the knowledge network known. It is furthermore used to raise customers' awareness of the network concept, since the customers should realize that they are members of an ongoing organizational structure.

In the HP support center case, the kick-off workshop was also used to identify more appropriate members for the knowledge network, since the company had invited several customers, who were considered trustworthy and knowledgeable, to attend. During the workshop the participants had the opportunity to decide if they wanted to participate.

The choice of HP representatives invited to attend was carefully planned in order to ensure their commitment to the knowledge network and its participants. For instance, the participation of HP's top management representatives illustrated the company's commitment to its customers as well as indicating its recognition of its customers' knowledge.

The structure of the kick-off workshop was furthermore aimed at creating a mutual understanding. Presentations were used to give the customers an understanding of a customer knowledge network and the mutual value to be gained from participation.

Besides the passive participation, an active part was also carried out. The group work session was aimed at enhancing the sense of belonging to a community, since the participants could create their own ideas and develop a group dynamic by developing the vision of the customer knowledge network. The customers were directly asked for their assistance as potential members of the knowledge network. They helped to answer the open questions and substantiated the knowledge network vision. The customers were addressed as IT professionals and potential members of the knowledge network, which gave them a sense of identification and self-esteem

The transition to the group work session was introduced by two questions, namely their motivation for cooperation and what the primary task and objectives of the knowledge network should be. The results from the interviews served as a background for the discussions. The participants had to place these results in order of priority and discuss them in a group with the final conclusions being presented to the other participants. HP representatives emphasized that these results were then part of the vision and would be communicated to the HP management.

However, one point of the reference model was ignored, namely the ICT tools. Therefore, at the end of this session, the third part of the reference model was mentioned and its important role as an enabler and supporter of knowledge sharing within a knowledge network was stressed. As an illustration that HP invested in such tools, a selection of the HP knowledge tools were shown to provide the customers with an overview of the tools used. The closure of the kick-off meeting aimed at once again motivating the customers and creating enthusiasm for the knowledge network through a summary of the obtained results and the further steps that needed to be undertaken. The customers then left the kick-off workshop with a task to be solved.

The kick-off workshop also aimed at delivering an actual knowledge network structure in which all participants interact and communicate with one another. This was achieved by the open discussions about the requirements and the group work session that enabled the creation of social ties between the customers.

Further Development of the Customer Network

In a following step, the network leader of the customer knowledge network created a detailed proposal for the customers to help them communicate the vision of the network to their companies and obtain their management's commitment. A communication plan, which comprised the results of the kick-off workshop, was also drawn up. A business plan, detailing the resources required and envisaged outcomes, was established in order to ensure the commitment of both the internal as well as the external management.

The kick-off workshop was the initial starting point of the HP customer knowledge network. The next step was for the knowledge network leader to create a closely-knit community from dissimilar participants. Before the knowledge network can enter a phase in which its performance can achieve the highest values, it is important to create a sense of belonging to the knowledge network through mutual value creation. This process can be depicted as a spiraling process in which the customers share their knowledge with the company and inspire the company representatives with new ideas and insights. These insights and new ideas lead to new or improved services that are delivered to the participants in the knowledge network. The new or improved services are then once more questioned by the participants and thereafter again deliver new insights and ideas.

This network first offered short-term incentives, but in time other motivational factors should replace "quick wins". HP's appreciation of their customers' knowledge was the first motivational factor for its customers to participate in the network. Succeeding tasks deliver enough incentives to act as continuous motivators to contribute to the knowledge network, as mentioned by the interviewees.

Supporting the Performance of the HP Customer Network

In order to develop and maintain the stability of the customer network, physical support is essential. Sponsors need to support the entire network with funding as well as funding further development. To maintain the social ties among the participants, regular communication forums with the customers are also needed. Furthermore, a communication channel has to be provided to connect the participants across the initiator company's borders in order to increase effective information exchange on the customer network's tasks and objectives.

In order to meet the above-described requirements, the HP representatives should continue to fund the customer knowledge network initiative. Face-to-face meetings have to be held often since they enable the transfer of implicit knowledge and maintain the social ties between the network members. Geographical dispersion of network members can be overcome by the ICT tools presented during the kick-off workshop.

Lessons Learned

One of the major findings relating to a knowledge network is that the initiative should have a strong link to the growth strategy of the company. The involvement and commitment of the top management are consequently essential to ensure strategic alignment and to provide resources and sponsorship for the network. In order to gain top management commitment, a business plan seems to be the appropriate means, especially if it discloses the values to be gained from the network and clarifies the required resources.

The initialization of a customer knowledge network requires the ascertaining of the prerequisites needed, like the potential challenges presented by the customers, their motivational aspects, their company background as well as the initiator company's competitors. This leads to a better initialization of a customer knowledge network.

Although informal, existing relationships enable a company to find leading-edge customers who can contribute their knowledge, the company representatives need to use their intuition in order to choose the appropriate customers. The appropriate composition of the group, i.e. they are not competitors, they speak the same language, and have the same needs, ensures an effective interaction and open communication during the meetings.

The company's representatives in the customer knowledge network ought to be people of a similar type. For instance, if the customers want to solve a technical problem in the network, the company representatives should have a technical background.

Customers appreciate that the company is listening to them. However, the customers' contribution of knowledge that the company will use in services and products, entails a quid pro quo situation – they want to see tangible and equivalent assets.

In order to ensure the appropriate outcomes, a management board, comprised of representatives from customer companies and from the initiator company should supervise the knowledge network initiative. This implies a communication of the network concept to both parties. In the case of HP, this issue was clarified before the set-up of the knowledge network.

General Recommendations

The following general recommendations ought to provide some practical insights into the set-up of an inter-organizational network with customers. The generalization of recommendations was possible through a constructive dialogue with companies' representatives facing similar situations.

- A company needs external knowledge integration in order to act and react to the environmental situations. By listening to the customers' experiences, a company can gain insights into latent requirements. It is therefore prudent to establish regular constructive dialogues. These might take the form of a knowledge network.

- In order to set up and maintain a customer network, visible top management support is essential. Top management support should begin before the initiation of the network and has to continue during the customer network's full life cycle.
- Company representatives ought to be open to criticism, and show customers their appreciation of the gained insights. They have to establish a regular and constructive dialogue with customers.
- Trust and mutual obligation are long-term tasks and not easily achieved, although acceleration can be achieved through existing relationships. A company willing to integrate customers has to identify existing relationships on which it can build a deeper involvement by the customers.
- Connections made through face-to-face meetings form the foundation of efficient cooperation. During this first meeting, the participants may recognize that they belong within the network and get to know other participants.
- The participants should have a common language and understand one another, although these features can not be guaranteed even when people are physically close, and are observing and discussing the same environment. However, appropriate participant selection, a shared environment and the opportunity to talk together do facilitate the cognitive dimension.

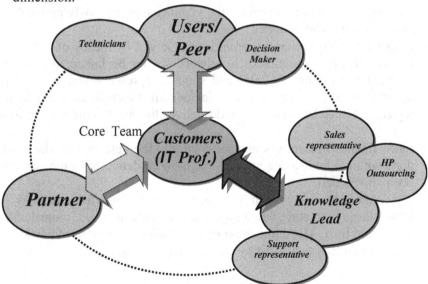

Fig. 3.2. Customer knowledge network structure

- A knowledge network leader is the central person in a customer knowledge network and should be a representative of the company that wants to establish the customer knowledge network. He should understand the external environment in which the company exists as well as the customers needs. He has to support the forming of a community from dissimilar participants through mutual value creation.
- To protect the customer network's quality of work, it needs to be gated. This means that only appropriate members ought to be selected and the selection should be based on the customers' existing relationships with the initiator company. The selection process can be facilitated if the customers and the company's representatives have common interests.
- Since the participants have different company backgrounds and use different terminologies, the first contact with all customers ought to ensure the cognitive, structural and relational dimension of social capital creation. In order to ensure the creation of social capital, the participants need an introduction to the customer knowledge network as well as being offered enough opportunities to express their own ideas and insights.
- The affiliation to the customer network is task-related. In order to facilitate the commitment of the customer network participants, the first objectives of a customer network ought to resemble low hanging fruit that can be reached quite easily. This is an appropriate approach with which to establish a reputation as a successful knowledge network and vital for the knowledge network's existence, since the short-term task may generate success faster and provide the viability that the newly established knowledge network requires.
- In order to gain advantages from a task solved by means of customer knowledge, the outcomes of a network should be linked to external functional lines such as sales and support representatives, and stakeholders. Since the network cannot include all stakeholders, it has to integrate the stakeholders who could deliver the most value for the network.
- Since financial incentives are not common, the outcomes of the work done within a knowledge network ought to be delivered to the customers involved first.
- The initiator company has to keep in mind that a knowledge network is a long-lasting structure based on the participants involved, mutual obligation and trust. The termination of an established customer knowledge network can lead to distrust by the company's customers.

4 Supporting Growth through Innovation Networks in Unilever

Maria Rumyantseva[1], Ellen Enkel[1] and Anita Pos[2]

[1]Research Center KnowledgeSource, University of St. Gallen, Switzerland
[2]Knowledge Management Group, Unilever N.V.

Abstract

Strong competition, market maturity and improvement in R&D practices led to the re-evaluation of strategic policies in many industries. These issues also caused a shift of emphasis from the conventional bottom-line sources of growth, aimed at increasing efficiency and profitability, to their re-combination with a top-line growth source, which ensures long-term competitiveness through innovations.

At Unilever, the focus on knowledge and innovations has a solid background, since knowledge management has been actively practiced in the company for the last 10 years and measurable results have been achieved. Currently, Unilever's five-year strategic plan announced in 2000 is "a series of linked initiatives designed to align entire organization behind ambitious plans for accelerating growth and expanding markets". This is to be achieved by "focusing on Unilever's leading brands and supporting them with strong innovation" ("Path to Growth", 2000).

Considering the company's rich experience in the area of innovation, the innovation network fits ideally into the current initiatives. It links local communities of practice, focused on the tacit knowledge dimension, with the innovation process management (IPM) program aimed at the coordination of the innovation initiatives across the company and dominantly focused on providing information and explicit sources of knowledge.

The tasks of the innovation network are to increase the transparency of existing innovation initiatives and increase the credibility of the company's innovation strategy through the direct involvement of employees in the process of selection and prioritization of projects.

The importance of the network for the company strategy, the high level of portfolio coordination that it is granted, and its structural links through the organizational matrix with units that are responsible for their own financial prosperity, imply the possibility of hidden agendas. These hidden agendas make the work of network more challenging, but simultaneously indicate that there is a real value at stake and that the professional management of the innovation network could produce real value for the company. Finally, we made some suggestions on the ways how this value could be monitored and quantified.[14]

The Launch of the Innovation Network

Conceptual Background

In the last decade, innovation has become one of the most important factors with which to achieve a competitive advantage. This has inspired a considerable amount of research as well as interest in the practice of improving the processes and outcomes of innovation activity (Christensen, 1997; Baden-Fuller, 1992; Drucker, 1991; Henderson and Clark, 1990; Kanter, 1988).

All companies in the market place have to deal with intense international competition, demanding and fragmented markets and the speed at which technological change is occurring. The traditional growth sources, such as risk minimization and increased efficiency, no longer assure sustainability of development. Today the major source of continuous growth is innovation, which, however, cannot be easily produced. Difficulties in stimulating innovation arise, first, due to the progressively changing environment. And, second, due to most companies' internal characteristics, which include structural inertia, path dependency and limited absorptive capacity. These problems have to be challenged in order to transform and adapt the company to the market and to produce relevant innovations (Levinthal and March, 1993; Cohen and Levinthal, 1990).

In such a complex situation, innovation cannot simply be produced by one or more company departments, e.g. R&D or marketing, in isolation. On the contrary, it should be co-produced by the whole company, since

[14] We are grateful for the insights from and the very constructive cooperation with Dr. Anita Pos, Dr. Manfred Aben and Dr. Bert van Wegen as well as other representatives of the Unilever Knowledge Management Group.

only a consolidated effort can lead to an adequate response to changes in the external environment and to the essential adjustment of internal structures. Before a company can learn from innovation, it must rethink the process by which innovation is transmitted throughout the organization. This means that departments throughout the company should co-produce new technologies, products and work practices by developing new processes and a shared understanding of why these innovations are important. In other words, in conditions of rapid and unpredictable change, the creation of individual products is in line with the creation of a general organizational aptitude for innovation (Brown, 2002).

Similar to this approach is the prioritization of company-wide or systemic innovations, created as a consistent chain of complementary innovations, which should replace autonomous, independent and, as a rule, incremental innovations (Henderson and Clark, 1990). Systemic innovations require longer lead times and the convergence of the different kinds of knowledge that are available in different departments. However, if these innovations are successful, the obtained new knowledge (Drucker, 2002) could serve as a basis for sustainable company growth.

The process of joint coordination and development of an innovation by the relevant company departments requires the exchange of a broad flow of both explicit and tacit knowledge. The latter denotes implicitly grasped knowledge that is not fully articulated, e.g., the know-how of a master craftsman, or the ingrained perspectives of a specific department. Because such knowledge is deeply embedded within individuals or departments, it tends to diffuse slowly and then only with the dedicated efforts and commitment of those involved (von Krogh et al., 2000).

Conventional organizational structures are often not prepared to support such a specific flow of knowledge, since they are aimed at formal interactions and are mainly, or only, judged by tangible or financial indicators. To support an increase in explicit and tacit knowledge flows, alternatives have to be introduced to conventional and hierarchical structures that offer different arrangements, processes, incentives and performance measurement systems.

Taking the above into consideration, an advantage of the network form – in contrast to hierarchical structures – is its flexibility and appreciation of innovation opportunities, while it – in contrast to decentralized teams – simultaneously has sufficient coordination power to support innovation (Teece, 1986).

Another important feature of the network form lies in the premise that a network reflects the interdependence between individuality and collectivity. In accordance with Giddens' (1984) notion of "duality of structure", there are no aspects of the social reality of networks that are completely independent of the influence of individuals. A network exists only in so far as it is constituted by individual actors and is implicated in an actor's motivation. Therefore, on the one hand, a network largely consists of individual interests, on the other hand, this allows the network to influence and manage individual perception and, therefore, create very high credibility for the process on which it is focused (Nooteboom, 1999).

Consistent with this reasoning, the network – through its focus on the human factor – is able to support the intangible aspects of systemic innovations in a way less applicable to a conventional organizational form (Powell, 1990).

Company Background

Unilever is an Anglo-Dutch consumer goods company with corporate centers in London and Rotterdam. With annual sales of approximately $48 billion, Unilever is one of the world's largest consumer product companies. It produces and sells a wide range of foods and home and personal care products that are known and trusted by millions of consumers around the world, including well-known brands such as Magnum ice cream, Dove, Omo, Flora, Hellmann's mayonnaise, Lipton tea and Knorr.

The company's strategy supports constant development, therefore about two per cent of annual turnover is invested in basic research and product innovations, leading to the filing of more than 400 patent applications annually. The very essence of the Unilever strategy is embodied in its "Path to Growth" – a strategic plan for the company's development that identifies priority areas and sets concrete growth numbers. To illustrate, Unilever has promised to both increase revenue by 5-6% per annum and reach a sustainable operating margin of 16%+ by 2004. It is committed to delivering double-digit earnings per share until 2004 and to ranking in the top third of its peer group in total shareholder return. The "Path to Growth" sets the strategy and identifies the funding with which to achieve this continued growth.

Consequently, in August 2000, Unilever announced the devolution of its management structure in order to increase efficiency and support its existing brand-name products. Two global divisions – one for Foods and one for Home & Personal Care (HPC) – were created. Regionally, these global divisions are organized into business groups. On a product basis, product categories are responsible for the implementation of Unilever's operations, and work closely with business groups to develop regional strategies. These product categories are also empowered to direct and manage the allocation of corporate R&D resources.

To ensure the success of its growth strategy, Unilever also obtained a number of acquisitions, one of which was a large international enterprise, BestFoods. Its geographical structure and products were merged with Unilever's business groups and product category structures, which initiated some changes in the relative weights of the categories. Among the recently reestablished product categories is Food Solutions, a large part of which has been acquired from BestFoods. Food Solutions is a fast growing category that caters to the professional market, serving as a supplier to fast food chains such as McDonalds as well as to independent restaurants, hospital kitchens etc. Although its sales volumes per product are small compared to the sales volumes of other product categories, this category is perceived to have a high potential for growth, which it is primarily expected to reach through a transition from a mainly local to a more European perspective on innovation. Initiatives that increase the transparency of knowledge processes and involve local units in cooperation on innovation creation will play an important role in Food Solutions' quest for top-line growth. These are ideal circumstances for the implementation of a new organizational approach such as an innovation network.

As Mr. Niall FitzGerald, Chairman of Unilever PLC, England, stated some time ago: "The Path to Growth is all about bringing together Unilever's knowledge, learning and understanding and applying it in a very focused way in the marketplace". In order to support knowledge processes in innovation, a single, common Unilever discipline, language and set of IT tools – collectively known as the Unilever IPM – was launched in 1997. The Unilever IPM, as a set of processes, and Inoplan (TM), as its IT tool, were developed to facilitate knowledge processes across product category and business group boundaries. They also simplified the decision making on innovation projects, partially delegating it to the business units and product categories. IPM is implemented worldwide and is designed to provide procedural clarity and information transparency to all Unilever employees involved in the innovation process. Currently Food Solutions has to complete the implementation of an IPM process and utilize it effectively.

The Knowledge Management Group (KMG) is an institution formed to make the best use of Unilever's available knowledge and to build new, business-related knowledge with which to achieve the company's growth objectives. Examples of knowledge management solutions that are offered by the KMG include organizational assessment of knowledge and knowledge enablers; workshops to locate, capture and share knowledge; the launch and maintenance of Communities of Practice (CoP)[15] etc. CoPs, which nurture the sharing and creation of knowledge that is key to the achievement of both company and personal objectives, play an important role in knowledge activities. CoPs usually consist of a core group of 10-12 members that may be increased by the inclusion of others in the same line of practice. Experienced in building and sustaining CoPs as well as in supporting other knowledge activities, the Knowledge Management Group is a partner in Food Solutions' transition from a mainly local to a more European orientation. Since Food Solutions' current, local innovation practices are fairly loosely coupled, the KMG has to implement a new organizational form of innovation network that is based on the CoP and is aimed at the coordination of the innovations on the product category level.

The Need for an Innovation Network

Food Solutions' Specific Situation

At the time of the IPM launch, the tactics in respect of innovation practices in Food Solutions were integrated and the category underwent a transition from differing global, regional and local perceptions of the R&D to a largely European perception. The innovation process, supported by IPM, has now been formalized on the senior levels where the nominal steering and decision-making functions occur. However, the coordination between the operational-level innovations and the higher-level consolidating form, frameworked by IPM, could be strengthened even further. Improved formal and, especially, informal ways of communication between the relevant local and European units could increase the transparency and credibility of the new innovation process and thus contribute to its efficiency. Ultimately, this will support the systemic character of innovation and its roll-outs.

The successful implementation of the innovation process in Food Solutions requires the use of all existing means to facilitate implementation. Besides the IPM, a specific portfolio-level form and instantiation of the CoP concept – an innovation network – was therefore suggested.

---

[15] The concept of communities of practice as used here does not correspond to the traditional understanding of a CoP as a self-emerging, informal organizational form (Wenger, 1998). These are more formal and deliberately launched forms with clearly defined goals and tasks that are directly aligned with other Unilever activities. Although these organizations methodologically meet the definition of knowledge networks, Unilever prefers the term CoP and it is used as such.

The Challenges Associated with the Power Structure

To better understand the challenge of small organizational forms within the company, it is advisable to understand those of larger forms first since the organizational structure of a company engenders considerable preconditions for any processes.

Unilever's history of fast expansion and numerous acquisitions of companies with related products, as well as the company's profile engender certain preconditions and require an organizational structure in the form of a global matrix. Like any other organizational form, the matrix form, successfully exploited by Unilever, does have its drawbacks. Particularly in the area of knowledge processes, the various units of the matrix form, so efficient at information transfer and adaptation, are much less focused on cooperation with other units. They do not have the time consuming and demanding personal interaction processes that tacit knowledge sharing requires. From this perspective, the units of the organizational matrix, which constitute, e.g., a product category, operate in parallel and could miss the specific advantages of sharing tacit knowledge, and therefore, an opportunity to accelerate innovation.

The bridging of "knowledge islands" is partially the task of the company's various communities of practice. Communities of practice are without a doubt an efficient tool with which to connect people from different units and with which to stimulate effective knowledge sharing and the creation of new ideas and valuable insights. However, as a tool for focusing on interpersonal communication and supporting formal organizational forms, communities of practices offer local or regional remedies and do not have sufficient authority or influence when other powers have to be considered.

Since all units in the matrix system are responsible for their own financial outcomes, this is a strong incentive for optimizing their processes and keeping improvements and the associated accumulated power to themselves. Such a power structure may lead to hidden agendas, which may negatively influence communities of practice's work.

The challenge of overcoming hidden agendas is obviously a point that is as applicable to an innovation network. And as the latter is closely connected to the strategic priorities of the company, and thus of its units, such hidden scenarios could well occur and even escalate in an innovation network. The network focuses on the most vulnerable asset – innovation – and the task of knowledge sharing and joint creation could partially contradict the existing entrepreneurial values of regions and units. Therefore, the possibility of "hidden agendas" is quite high in the Innovation Network and need to be addressed.

Another issue that arises from the company's structure, and is related to these hidden agendas, is the degree to which the network should be empowered. On the one hand, empowering the network might increase the fear of losing power locally and could therefore support the network members' hidden agendas. On the other hand, a network with no power might be too unattractive for potential members. This would mean the demotivation of the existing network members, and that the corporate innovation values that Unilever are aiming at wouldn't be sufficiently delivered. This question therefore needs to be addressed by means of the choice of sufficiently empowered network structure and clearly identified goals and tasks for the network.

The last issue, which is as important as those pointed out above, is the measurement of the network performance. This point is strongly related to the goals of the network and the value it has to provide for the company and the regions. It is quite clear that the measures applied for the measuring of the Unilever CoPs will not be suitable for an innovation network. The outcome of the innovation network needs to complement the IPM and general innovation process outcomes.

Illustrating the value of the innovation network will influence the top management support as well as the motivation of the network's members. Only if the right values can be created, will the necessary motivation be in place. On the other hand, appropriate performance measures are crucial to monitor this new organization form within Unilever and adapt it if necessary. The performance measurement issue, as well as other critical issues mentioned, are to be addressed in the section on the project results.

Approach Taken by the Research Project

In order to visualize the approach taken by the project, let us now take a closer look at the company's processes, particular those dealing with innovations. The company's global matrix structure could lead to innovation processes on the corporate, regional and country levels having unrealized potential for better coordination. Being aware of this, the management of Unilever launched and consistently promotes the Innovation Process Management (IPM) program, which is aimed at the efficient coordination of all innovation initiatives occurring in the company. Due to its clear procedures, visible structure and constant promotion by top management, the program is appreciated on all organizational levels.

As a company-wide, formal program, IPM serves, among others, as a well-tuned coordination mechanism. However, practiced routines and incremental approaches to the innovation process, particularly those in the recently acquired companies, may remain hidden. They could reside deep in individual perceptions and require different processes to deal with them.

There are currently mixed approaches to innovation: there are calls for centralization from the top and, sometimes, observed residual practices could blur the individual understanding of the direction that should be taken. As a consequence, priorities and the values on individual, country and regional levels are sometimes unclear. To resolve this state of affairs, the company should focus on the tacit aspects of the current situation, and on ways to reach high identification with and credibility of the corporately prioritized processes.

The great role played by tacit aspects should also be acknowledged in the innovation process itself. IPM, as a part of the formal organizational structure and with a significant part of its communication made by means of information technologies, may not cover all tacit aspect of the innovation process. Particularly those requiring longitudinal and carefully managed cooperation could be advanced. For the tacit dimension to be adequately supported there should be additional organizational forms. The one organizational form that fits this description is an innovation network.

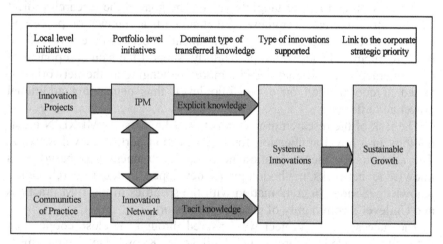

Fig. 4.1 The role of the Innovation Network in the Unilever innovation strategy and process

As indicated in the above figure, the formalized innovation process stems from innovation projects' background and is embodied in the form of the IPM. The organizational form parallel to it is an innovation network, which has had CoPs as its prototype. Consistent with this background, it is strongly focused on the tacit dimensions of the innovation process, namely interpersonal coordination, as well as all the specific characteristics of a

CoP. As is also indicated in Fig. 4.1, an innovation network is purely focused on the innovation process and, similar to the IPM, operates primarily on the upper – portfolio – organizational level. What distinguishes it from local communities, is that it is focused on only one of the areas of the company's activities.

As an innovation network is aimed at operating on country, regional and global levels, it obviously has to make a distinct, tangible and very visible contribution to the innovation process in order to justify its existence. Therefore the innovation network tasks include assisting with the creation of process transparency, credibility and ensuring that the created valuable business innovations are acknowledged and pushed through production and placed on the market. The process transparency could play a prominent role by reducing redundancies and providing a basis for cooperation and synergies. Clearly formulated tasks are, of course, the solution to half of the problem. Now the best way for the network to achieve these tasks should be found.

Examining how an innovation network could support innovation processes, and therefore contributing to the innovative ability and growth of Unilever, seemed to be of tangible value. The goal of the research project was therefore to create a framework that supports an innovation process in general as well as supporting the communication between the involved innovating members and would, particularly, support the tacit component of such interactions. The goal became more challenging as the network was aimed at coordination on a portfolio level, thus demanding additional power and effort.

The task of the research project was to test the existing MERLIN methodology in a novel application for an innovation portfolio-level network. The scenario for the innovation network development was based on a knowledge networks methodology as developed at the research center KnowledgeSource, in combination with the specifics of the IPM practices and Unilever's community of practice framework.

The success of the project was ensured through the close cooperation between KnowledgeSource and Unilever's Knowledge Management Group.

Multiple sources were used for data collection to adapt the knowledge network framework to the particular goal of increasing innovation and to the company's specifics such as, e.g., its structure and culture. During the project the authors had access to internal company documents, archival data and intranet resources which helped with the adequate adaptation of the model. For a better grasp of the situation, semi-structured interviews were conducted with interviewees selected to represent the geographical and functional diversity within Food Solutions Europe and one with a company employee from Food Solutions Global. The project included ten days of on-site joint work, a two-day workshop and comprised a total duration of six months.

The Development of the Innovation Network

In the present section we will concentrate on the methodology of network development and will particularly focus on the distinctive features of an innovation network, which either differ from the MERLIN methodology or support it. Generally, an innovation network requires all the methodological steps identified by MERLIN. On the levels of the facilitating conditions, knowledge processes and knowledge network architecture we selected various differences, which are presented in the following subsections of this section.

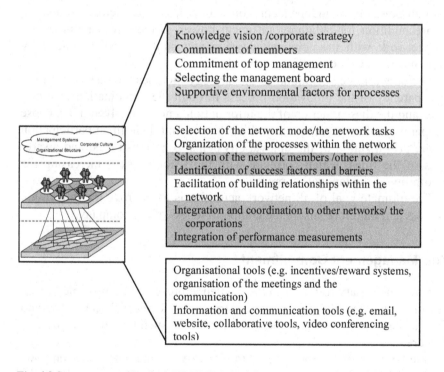

Knowledge vision /corporate strategy
Commitment of members
Commitment of top management
Selecting the management board
Supportive environmental factors for processes

Selection of the network mode/the network tasks
Organization of the processes within the network
Selection of the network members /other roles
Identification of success factors and barriers
Facilitation of building relationships within the
  network
Integration and coordination to other networks/ the
  corporations
Integration of performance measurements

Organisational tools (e.g. incentives/reward systems,
organisation of the meetings and the
communication)
Information and communication tools (e.g. email,
website, collaborative tools, video conferencing
tools)

Fig. 4.2 Steps suggested by the MERLIN Methodology

There are components of a network structure that need to be adapted specifically for an innovation network since they summarize the challenges the innovation network has to face and the values it should create – as mentioned in the previous section. These are (as marked in the above figure): alignment with the company's growth strategy, ensuring the top management and network members' commitment, which includes building relationships within the network and with the rest of the organization, identifying supporting environmental factors and organizational tools to support the network action, which will include appropriate performance measurement to illustrate the network's value.

Alignment with the Company's Vision and Corporate Strategy

The level of network empowerment is a critical question. An innovation network as a portfolio-level organizational form supporting a tangible and difficult manageable interpersonal cooperation process, has to possess enough power to be independent from numerous contradictory influences. A precondition for obtaining sufficient power, is the direct alignment of the network with the company's vision and strategy, which practically guarantees the existence of the network.

The network's contribution to the strategy includes the task of creating transparency of the innovation process through the coordination of initiatives and the dissemination of the information among involved units. Close cooperation of employees from different units and their direct participation in the prioritization of the innovations helps to establish trust and awareness of the rules, which correlate with the second task – increasing the credibility of the innovation process.

The ultimate goal of all network activities is to improve the innovation process and therefore ensure the competitiveness of the company.

Top Management Commitment

It is now necessary to return to the challenge presented by possible hidden agendas related to the specific power structure of Unilever's categories and the question to what extent the network and its members need to be empowered.

One solution to this problem is to clarify what the network is empowered to do and what not. The question in line with this thought is that if the network is given power, how much individual power does the network members need in order to create value? In other words, is it necessary to choose network members who are high on the hierarchical level to ensure that they have sufficient personal power to ensure the successful transfer of the network results to the regional units and to enable the network to make decisions? Or could the selection of members with much personal power, due to their function within the matrix organization, be seen as a precondition for conflicts of power within the network, ultimately resulting in no value being created at all?

The answer is that a network apparently needs more power than a CoP, since it functions on a higher level and deals with the sensitive issue of innovation. To ensure a higher degree of power, the top management's genuine interest and commitment should be gained through the innovation network's strategic relevance. This will also allow lower-level employees to devote time to network participation.

Selection and Motivation of the Network Members

Since the network focuses on innovations, its membership should primarily consist of R&D representatives as long as other functions are not directly involved in the first stages of network development. The innovation network could include a limited number of middle management representatives, and be mostly represented by researchers and practitioners. However, all these members should be key figures in the R&D in their units.

The innovation network's emphasis is on the coordination of people. Its participants' motivation will therefore be critical. As one of the interviewees stated, the network should deliver "compelling innovations" as "others join if they are convinced, not if they are talked into joining". To a certain extent, employees are isolated from one another and would actually like closer interaction. Besides this motivating factor, they realize that individually they cannot innovate effectively, therefore successful collaborative work could motivate them to join the network. These motivations are all related to an increase in efficiency and are closely connected with personal incentives such as individual working time that can be saved, recognition by colleagues, increased trust and confidence in the work etc.

Supportive Environmental Factors for Knowledge Processes

Company-internal environmental factors influencing an innovation network play a very influential role at Unilever. In terms of the project we saw numerous evidences of how the company's background influences the innovation network development in both indescribable and tangible ways. The Unilever case has provided a large number of positive connections between the network development and the company's practices, but we also encountered a few factors that could potentially impede network operations.

Besides the overall stimulating atmosphere for innovation development, two practices were especially supportive for the development of an innovation network. These are the IPM as a more formalized support for innovation processes, running parallel with the innovation network, and the CoP experiences in the company that substantially facilitated the justification of an innovation network.

Distinct Success Factors and Barriers

The prevalence of individual interests and possible conflicts of power are considered common to all large multinational companies. The probability of these hidden agendas appearing during the network launch is therefore quite high and constitutes one of the barriers.

A precondition for the network's success is a clear structure for the company's innovation process. Such a formal structure determines the role the network will play when new, cross-boundary innovations are proposed.

At Food Solutions the structure of the innovation process is aimed at the delivery of major innovations per country. Europe-wide, the network functions should primarily be comprised of coordination and project prioritizing, which will support the IPM and influence the long-term innovation policy.

Another important precondition is a clear definition of the network processes. The latter is dependent on the short- to middle-term tasks that the network has to achieve.

Tasks of the Innovation Network

The interviews conducted within Food Solutions helped us to identify concrete tasks in line with the proclaimed general tasks of creating transparency and credibility.

The tasks denoted in Fig. 4.2 will follow the described order. Starting with the generation of an overview of the projects, which supports transparency, the next step is harmonizing the process, prioritizing projects and specifying ideas for future projects, which further increases the credibility of the process for the participants. Finally, additional transparency is gained by the dissemination of accumulated information through category and external monitoring.

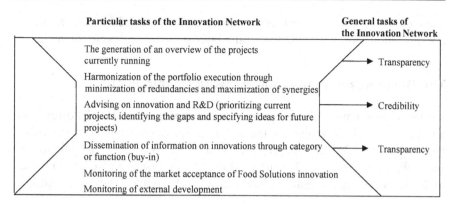

Fig. 4.3 General vs. particular tasks of the Innovation Network

Integration of Performance Measurement

For an evaluation of the innovation network's performance, we suggested quantifying the results in two ways. First, through monitoring criteria that have been designed to keep track of a network's progress until the real deliverables can be proved. These criteria support the monitoring of the network's dynamics by measuring the number of innovation projects per region, country, and on a global level; measuring the number of projects in each phase of the project development, e.g., idea generation, feasibility and launch. The number of innovation rollouts, and the total number of overlapping projects are also significant criteria.

The second way of quantifying results is by identifying the deliverables of the network that contribute directly to the company's performance, which include both financial and qualitative indicators. Such indicators could, for example, be the speed with which the innovation moves from being an idea to its market distribution, the number of countries in which a new innovation is launched, and, ultimately, the growth achieved through innovation.

Organizational Tools

In the light of the limited involvement of functions other than R&D and those functions connected with it, additional sharing mechanisms should be set up for cross-functional sharing, both on a senior level and on more operational levels. In the Food Solutions network, innovation exchange events have already been agreed upon as a means of encouraging sharing between functions. Further mechanisms are also planned for further incorporation in the innovation network at a later stage of its development.

The Dynamics of Innovation Network Development

Unilever's long and rich background in the exploitation of CoPs offered us an opportunity to hypothesize the possible development path of the innovation network. Assuming that an innovation network is an instantiation of the CoP, allows us to predict many of its characteristics as well as to better understand the mechanisms of how it can create transparency and credibility.

Phases	I Start	II Community of Practice	III Network of Networks	IV Innovation Network
Source of Growth	-	efficiency (bottom-line growth)	efficiency (bottom-line growth)	innovation (top-line growth)
Major Purpose of the Phase	Build **trust/ relationships**	enable **knowledge sharing** among experts	support **coordination on portfolio** level, achieve synergies	enable **cooperation, between portfolios/regions** aimed at joint development of new processes and services

Fig. 4.4 Phase model of the innovation network development

The path, which leads from the CoP to the innovation network could, in a very abstract form, be presented by four phases. Such separation of phases does not mean that all phases take place, it is primarily aimed at showing the distinct components from which the innovation network is constructed.

The first phase, common to all communities or networks, is cultivating an atmosphere of trust, and maintaining mutual respect and friendly relationships between the members.

The second phase, typical of CoP activities, is intensive knowledge sharing between the involved experts.

However, if, in a third phase, the CoP topic excites the interests of a local group and the community transforms into a portfolio-level network, its first task simply becomes the general coordination of explicit knowledge and synergies through the alignment of redundant practices. To some extent this portfolio-level phase is similar to the first local-level phase, as it is aimed at building trustworthy relations between members sharing information, in order to start the more personal process of sharing knowledge.

During the fourth phase, which we called the innovation network, trust is created and the members are on the way to openly sharing their knowledge with one another. This will stimulate the transparency of the process and, through mutual trust, create credibility of the joint actions and the innovation process in general.

Analyzing the similarities between CoPs and an innovation network, it becomes obvious that the former predicts the form and development of the latter. Generalizing this fact, it can be legitimately said that the company's experiences with both CoPs and innovation programs made it possible to predict the tasks, structural characteristics and dynamics of the innovation network development.

The Corporate Advantage of a Web of Innovation Networks – Taking a Future Perspective

From a corporate perspective, building a web of independent innovation networks could gain the company significant corporate advantages. If the innovation network is successful in one product category, it might gain more value if combined with similar organizational structures in other categories, since synergies could possibly be created between differently profiled innovation networks within the same company. The minimum synergy of such a web of networks could be in sharing the network exploitation experience with the maximum value being achieved through mutual sharing of knowledge and creation of innovation. The possible antithesis is that once the network on the product category level has gained sufficient value, combining it with other innovation networks on a higher level and larger scale could endanger the gained value. The specifics of internal network interaction and the sensitivity that is required for the cultivation of a network atmosphere could endanger the whole endeavor.

Lessons Learned

The lessons learned during the action part of the project as well as during the various stages comprise a large list of insights, part of which, to a larger or smaller extent, could be generalized for other companies as well.

Among the generalizable lessons we would like to specify the most important ones.

Goal and Tasks

- The ultimate goal of the network is to contribute to the company's performance and growth by stimulating innovation processes on a portfolio level. All activities occurring in the network should be made with consideration of their value for the firm's profitability and competitiveness.
- The primary task of the network on its way to stimulate innovation is to ensure transparency of the innovation process. This is achieved by means of interpersonal communication aimed at the generation of information, its selection and further dissemination in the units.
- An equally important task is to increase the credibility of the innovation process. This is achieved by involving employees from different units in the joint selection and prioritization of the innovation projects. The mutual cooperation in the network implies an awareness of the rules of the selection process and helps to build an atmosphere of trust among those involved in the interaction. The implications are reflected in the units where the network participants work, ensuring overall credibility for the innovation process.

The Innovation Network and the Company

- The innovation network can only be successful if it is aligned with the company's values and strategy. If the company does not respect innovation as a strategic goal, the management's empowerment of the network to work on the portfolio level can not be guaranteed.
- The network on its own can not reach the goal of improving the innovation process due to its strong focus on the intangible aspects of the process, e.g. building trust among participants, and the limited number of members involved. In the innovation process the network therefore plays an important, but not the only, role.
- During the project we encountered numerous evidences of how a company's background influences the innovation network's development in both subtle and quite tangible ways. The company's background in the innovation process and its network exploitation, whether positive, neutral or negative, should be considered.

The Innovation Network from within

- The nature of the innovation process implies the involvement of many uncontrollable aspects, and the final outcome in the form of innovation can not always be appropriately safeguarded. It should always be considered that those involved in the network might have certain interests as well as hidden agendas.
- An innovation network as a portfolio-level organization should be given a certain power to balance its structure and the network processes should be prescribed.

Emphasis on R&D

- The membership of the innovation network, though logically encompassing representatives of the R&D, could be extended to any other employees involved in the innovation process.

Measurement of the Network Performance

- Finally, the outcomes of the network are an extremely important indicator of the justification of a network in the company. The nature of the outcomes, derived through the cooperation of several organizational forms, i.e. with the IPM, makes it difficult to allocate contributions to the network. However, both the innovation process indicators and outcome indicators should mirror the input of the innovation network.

General Recommendations

In an attempt to further generalize the findings to other companies, we identified a number of the Unilever categories' features that predefine the innovation network development. These features were classified into structural and procedural elements:

Company Structure

- The size of the company
- Centralized or decentralized company structure
- The formality of the hierarchy
- The amount of cross-category leverage required
- Whether there are links to innovations in the external world (e.g. suppliers or partners or customers)

Innovation Practice

- The type of innovation (e.g. product, service, or process)
- Characteristics of the central organizational driver (e.g. customer, marketing, R&D, or none)
- The amount of higher-management involvement or influence
- The number of functions involved in the innovation process, and the variation in the functions' involvement over time
- External parties' involvement in the innovation process
- The company or division's innovation maturity/background

Some of these features are already present in the Unilever case (e.g. company maturity/background in innovation process), while others have been fixed beforehand. To make the above list more tangible, some of the points will be specified. For better understanding we will also draw comparisons with the similar experiences in two international companies whose representatives provided inputs during the final discussions of the Unilever case results.

Among the structural elements, let's take the example of "company size": in a small company, setting up a network will be much easier and more informal than in a larger company. The latter requires time a consuming search and coordination of the right people inside the company, as well as stakeholder support for the innovation initiatives. International companies, such as Unilever and Hewlett Packard, also experience geographical barriers, including time zone differences, use of a number of languages etc. A large company tends to shift its communication towards a virtual environment, which limits the social component and raises alternative problems for the innovation process implementation.

Another example of the structural elements influencing Innovation Network development is the "link to innovations in the external world", e.g. of suppliers or customers. Unilever, for instance, checks consumer opinions both in respect of existing products and products under development. Hewlett Packard has established a "human factor group", which includes a range of customers invited to examine new ideas every two months in a joint collaboration project.

Among the structural elements of innovation practice, "type of innovation" will dictate the structure and the membership of the network: product, service or process innovation will require quite different levels of flexibility and the involvement of different functions. The evidence from the information technologies industry, using Hewlett Packard as an example, also indicates that product, service and process types of innovations are close linked in this industry and have to be exploited considerably faster in comparison with traditional manufacturing industries.

"Maturity/background of the company in the area of innovation" also plays a significant role. It predetermines coordination abilities on regional and global levels. At Unilever, innovation became the highest priority quite a while ago, but despite its successful implementation, the heritage of the company, comprised of a number of companies pooled together, is still sometimes tangible. Conversely, the innovation factor at Hewlett Packard was stressed from the time of company's founding and it is now part of the corporate culture. The German energy company RWE, facing the recent deregulation of the market, has started to focus on innovations and has had to develop its innovation practices from scratch.

To summarize: the Unilever case provides insights into an innovation network – a social structure supporting the innovation process parallel with conventional organizational structures. The primary attention of an innovation network is focused on the people involved and the process of cooperation and knowledge creation and the transfer between them. This could lead to the synergies through both the formal and informal structure of the Innovation Network mutually working together.

Looking into the future, it would be interesting to draw a comparison between the innovation networks in other companies, which will help to further build and validate the innovation network model.

5 A Methodology for Adapting Knowledge Networks – Managerial Guidelines

Ellen Enkel, Grzegorz Gurgul and Maria Rumyantseva

Research Center KnowledgeSource, University of St. Gallen, Switzerland

Introduction

The question of how one can adapt knowledge networks for individual business needs was raised and explained by means of three cases taken from practice. The following section will provide practitioners such as knowledge managers, network managers and the relevant knowledge management members with insights, examples and guidelines which help to build knowledge networks that will address their specific business needs.

Although the nature of this topic largely excludes providing guidelines for all possible structures of all possible knowledge networks to fulfill all business needs, this problem is solved by providing a general process description as derived from the research on knowledge networks for growth. Every step of an action is explained with examples from the three fields that we examined: customer integration networks, innovation networks, and merger & acquisition networks. The steps need to be followed in the order described, since one section builds logically on the previous section. Small cases, additional examples and the design of the guidelines will help you to understand and build knowledge networks for growth.

The structure of the following guidelines comprises three main parts: 1) the vision and strategy, 2) development of a roadmap and 3) the setting up of the network. First, the vision and strategy part discusses the preconditions required for knowledge networks for growth in your company vision and what your strategy should be from a knowledge perspective.

Based upon this, the development of a roadmap will be discussed in the second part. This includes the identification of processes and tasks that need to be supported with knowledge activities to follow your growth strategy, a stakeholder analysis, and the identification of both the knowledge needed and the existing knowledge, which will conclude with a decision to set up a knowledge network or not. If a network seems to be the appropriate way to address your business needs, the selection of a network reference mode needs to be done and the expected deliverables determined.

The third part includes the actual steps to set up a knowledge network for growth: from the identification of specific network goals and tasks to the development of a communication plan, the composition of a management board and factors to facilitate management commitment. The facilitation of the relationships within and outside the network will be discussed as well as the organization of the network members and meetings. The third part ends with the establishment of the internal performance measurement, which will be explained in detail in the article following these guidelines. The following figure illustrates the main steps for setting up your knowledge network for growth.

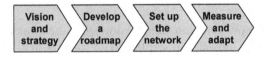

Fig. 5.1 Steps to set up knowledge networks for growth

To facilitate orientation, the above arrows will appear above the main part of the step in which you're actually working, with the relevant arrow highlighted. All steps are structured in exactly the same way:

- First the topic is briefly introduced.
- Answers are thereafter provided under the heading "Why this is important" and are indicated by a light bulb.
- Three sections from the fields: innovation, customer integration and merger & acquisition integration illustrate the specific challenges of this step for the specific field, since each requires a different network structure. These examples should help to identify your specific challenges and the adaptation needed to fulfill your business needs.
- The "steps to get you there" are indicated by a staircase. This describes the single steps required to implement this network component in your company. These components need to be adapted in keeping with your company specifics and according to the growth field that you want to support with your knowledge networks. To help you gather data and identify elements for adaptation, additional examples are given at the

end of some of these steps. In addition, specific templates to facilitate your work can be found in the appendix of this book.

As a last annotation after the measure and adapt part, you'll find a project plan with all the steps in the correct order and with an indication of the time the specific step may require. This project plan will give you an overview of the work required to set up a knowledge network for growth and will help you to apply these guidelines.

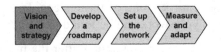

Vision and Strategy

This section conceptualizes the role of vision and strategy in emphasizing current knowledge activities and provides an outlook for their further development. The knowledge vision and strategy legitimize knowledge activities, and provide a platform for the launch of knowledge-supporting organizational forms. Besides focusing the vision and strategy on growth, other factors are important as well.

Vision

"Be the change you want to see around you" Gandhi

A vision provides a sense of and direction for the company's development, both in the present and in the future. The future prospect depends heavily on the company's current vision and is closely related to the knowledge vision, which is focused on the company's future performance and success. The formulation of the vision, particularly the knowledge vision, is based on establishing a connection between the current state of the company and the desired state in the future (see von Krogh et al., 2000, p.117). A vision can be best formulated made by answering the questions below:

- What is the current condition of the company?
- What is the desired condition of the company?

 **HP's Vision**

The current HP policy of encouraging a close relationship with its customers is precisely expressed in the company's vision and has been shaped by two basic beliefs. First, "we believe the reason HP exists is to satisfy real customer needs" and, second, "we believe those needs can be fully satisfied only with the active participation and dedication of everyone in the company". To give a sense of direction to these beliefs, HP suggests the means by which they may be achieved: "we must listen attentively to our customers to understand and respond to their current needs and to anticipate their future needs."

The materialization of the HP vision has led to the "Total Customer Experience" program, which is aimed at cooperation with customers, sharing the experience derived from the daily work with HP equipment and, ultimately, the creation of new services and products which could anticipate future customer needs.

On the corporate level, the vision is reflected in HP's transformation from a product-centric company to a customer-centric organization or, using the HP slogan, a "customer-obsessed company".

Slogans that sharply characterize the company's current and future business penetrate the employees' work intangibly and shape the unique and very strong HP culture. In fact, many of the slogans and particularly the vision do include a company knowledge vision. A knowledge vision could also be expressed in various other forms, such as in a mission statement, in a set of corporate values, or in the company's strategic outline. Managers can either communicate a knowledge vision by explicitly separating it, or they can integrate ideas on knowledge into other corporate statements (Rumyantseva et al. 2001).

Creating a Knowledge Vision

The knowledge vision is a picture of the knowledge the company produces and is looking for. The purpose of the vision is to generate a certain knowledge activity level to achieve desired goals, for example, company growth.

Why this is important:

- Understanding competitive market trends is essential for the perception of knowledge as a possible main source of company growth.
- Defining a knowledge vision means an analysis of the present, a view of the future and suggestions of ways to reach the latter. The vision, therefore, forms the roadmap for the company's development.
- Making the vision flexible allows for new insights from employees and stimulates them to continually revise the connection between the current state of the company, the technological opportunities available and the external environment.

Innovation

- There should be a strong alignment with the corporate vision and a long-term strategy asserting that innovation and knowledge are important or main sources of growth.
- The knowledge vision implies identification of the balance between the internal innovation process and outsourcing.
- To effectively outsource innovation, there should be a willingness to cooperate with external parties, such as customers, suppliers and competitors.
- A company-wide coordinated and transparent approach to innovation needs to be defined and communicated.
- A corporate innovation policy is defined on the upper organizational level and is then implement on the lower levels, often in the form of projects, focused on certain innovation activities. This link between policy makers and executors is sometimes blurred.

Customer Integration

- The strategic link between customer involvement and company development or growth should be seen and made explicit in the vision.
- Customers should be perceived as a source of knowledge that is necessary to create and sustain a competitive advantage.
- Customers want to share their knowledge, but they are not always sure where to start – be a facilitator to gain customers' knowledge.

Mergers & Acquisition Integration

- Acquiring new external knowledge is an important reason for mergers and acquisitions to take place. Consequently, the knowledge integration after M&A needs to be planned carefully and be aligned with the vision.

Steps to get you there:

1. Decide which people you want to involve when developing the vision (top-down, bottom-up, or middle up - top down).
2. Think of the current condition of the company: Which sources of growth dominate? What technologies are used? What kind of expertise do we have to maintain the company's sustainable competitive advantage?
3. What are the gaps? What knowledge do the organizational members need to have or create to bridge the gaps?
4. Think of the desired condition of the company: Is it possible to merge current technologies or expertise? Are there possible novel sources of growth?
5. Think of what kind of knowledge is needed by the organizational members to achieve the future world in which you want to live. What kind of knowledge do we have to acquire or develop?
6. Formulate an open-ended vision.

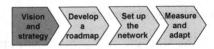

Identify Your Knowledge Strategy

The vision of the company should be reflected in its strategy. Since the vision identifies current gaps and points out the direction that the development should take, the strategy operationalizes it in the form of short-term and long-term goals towards reaching the desired condition. Linking knowledge activities to a strategy is crucial. There must be a consistent knowledge management focus on business value. The alignment of the knowledge actions with overall strategic goals that all business units find sound, ensures that locally too there will be efforts to help fulfil the company strategy. Furthermore, the prudent choice of a single strategic goal to be followed forms the foundation for selecting a business process or task, and for choosing the appropriate knowledge activities. But what business goals should be our focus when managing knowledge for company growth?

Companies pursue three basic business goals to reach growth, namely risk optimization, improvement in efficiency and an increase in innovation.

Risk optimization: We need to share and create knowledge in specific fields to reduce our risks.

Improvement in efficiency: We need to improve our efficiency by transferring knowledge to crucial fields and need to create required knowledge with which to refine our internal processes.

An increase in innovation: To increase our innovation rate we need to share existing knowledge and create new knowledge as a prerequisite for developing new products and services.

Generally, a knowledge strategy can be divided into two parts:

- **survival strategy**, in which the company concentrates its knowledge efforts on maintaining its current level of success and performance; and
- **advancement strategy** that emphasizes future success and improved performance.

While risk optimization and improvement of efficiency are primarily related to the survival strategy, an increase in innovation is more related to the advancement strategy. The latter could also be achieved by increasing the attention paid to internal knowledge and innovation practices as well as to external sources of innovation such as technological standards, formation of strategic alliances, or by building strong links with suppliers and customers.

In the current competitive environment, the priority of the innovation process is obvious. However, balancing the survival and advancement strategies is necessary to fulfill the ultimate goal of the knowledge strategy: to ensure above average industry profitability for a company, both in the short and long term.

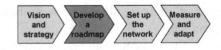

Develop a Roadmap

The purpose of this section is to obtain an understanding of what knowledge is available from which sources, what the required relevant knowledge is with which to meet the strategic goal and whether a network is the correct option with which to achieve this.

The development of a roadmap includes the identification of processes and tasks that need to be supported by knowledge activities in order to follow your growth strategy, a stakeholder analysis and the identification of required and existing knowledge. These activities will conclude with a decision to establish a knowledge network or not. If a network seems to be an appropriate way of addressing your business needs, the selection of a network reference mode has to be done and the expected deliverables have to be defined.

Select a Process or Task that You Want to Support and Understand

In order to meet the strategic goal identified in the previous section, knowledge activities should be focused on a concrete business process or task. More precisely, they should be focused on a knowledge gap or the leveraging of the existing knowledge activities that characterize this process or task.

Why this is important:

- If the selected process is linked to the strategy, it will contribute to the overall goal of company growth.
- Understanding the processes allows you to focus on the project without losing sight of the big picture.
- Only when you understand when and where people need to act, and thus require knowledge, can you understand what kind of knowledge and what kind of knowledge activity are needed.

Innovation

- A coordinated and transparent company-wide innovation process needs to be prepared and communicated at this stage.
- However, the power of an innovation process is often local, for instance, in the catering industry the greatest volume of innovation is produced on department or subsidiary levels, therefore local initiatives should be carefully considered.
- At the same time, local innovation initiatives should be in line with the company-wide innovation process and core competencies.

Customer Integration

- Create a strong link between the process and the corporate strategy: customers' knowledge integration can both increase corporate efficiency by providing the right products and services, and, more importantly, support corporate innovation by integrating a new and valuable source of knowledge.
- Trust customers, listen carefully and incorporate their knowledge through defined processes such as customer events, frequent interviews and the integration of customers in knowledge networks.

Mergers & Acquisition Integration

- A lack of knowledge or skills is an important reason for an M&A, therefore it is crucial to clarify which knowledge is lacking in your company and which knowledge and skills the acquired entity has that you need to integrate.
- Create appropriate conditions and processes for knowledge integration.

 Steps to get you there:

1. Examine your knowledge vision, your strategy, and the business objectives that you aim to achieve. These three factors will help you identify a selection of business processes or tasks.
2. Identify business needs through an analysis of the existing practices or routines, and decide what knowledge you require to meet these needs.
3. Specify the gap that you want to close with the knowledge activities.
4. Select one business process or task that you want to support with knowledge activities and describe the new process or task that your knowledge activities have to perform.

Perform a Stakeholder Analysis

The purpose of the stakeholder analysis is to provide an understanding of the needs, priorities, and ideas for action to those who will influence the success of your knowledge management initiatives. We can distinguish between two groups of stakeholders, namely internal and external. The internal group includes senior managers, functional and staff support groups, internal clients at various levels and others. The external group consists of the key external partners, such as customers, suppliers, competitors, dealers, universities, consultants and others.

Why this is important:

- The stakeholder analysis forms the foundation for an evaluation of the chosen business process or task that you identified in the previous step. Do the stakeholders regard this chosen process as important for obtaining company growth, and do they see potential for improving it through knowledge management activities?
- Through the involvement of the stakeholders, you minimize the risk of incorrect action and you help to reinforce commitment to your new knowledge activities.
- It therefore is very important to analyze stakeholders' opinions and raise interest in your activity.
- Finally, the stakeholder analysis is important as a prerequisite for later obtaining sponsors for the activities.

Innovation

- Innovation initiatives should be discussed and accepted by senior management.
- Important stakeholders are R&D representatives as well as marketing, sales, and supply chain management. External sources like universities or research centers may be also important to ensure the external flow of knowledge.
- Take care to integrate regional, global and functional stakeholders, depending on your innovation initiative's location.
- Ensure that you know who will be the "owner" of the result and who will maintain the process.

Customer Integration

- Because of their strong link to strategy, it is important to take care of stakeholders in the top management.
- Other stakeholder might be the company customer support and marketing functions due to their contact with customers.
- Customers are important stakeholders as well.
- Customers are one of the most valuable assets a company has, therefore consider the corporate identity: How would your company like to be presented at meetings or in communication with customers? What is the mission you want to communicate?
- Before talking to customers or raising initiatives, ensure that you have carefully planned and discussed your approach with all stakeholders. Don't spoil customers' willingness to share their knowledge with trivial or carelessly planned initiatives.

Mergers & Acquisition Integration

- Besides the top management and the integration managers, you should pay attention to the managers of the reorganized business units where you want to start your integration initiative.
- Knowledge integration should follow a top-down approach with strong involvement by integration managers. Keep in mind that the situation after a merger or an acquisition is often characterized by uncertainty (fear of losing jobs, trusting of top management etc.)
- In a post-merger phase, during which knowledge network initiatives first start making sense, be careful when communicating with stakeholders. They might be stressed as a result of the many changes during the M&A, or may have lost power during the reorganization, or are still lost in the atmosphere of uncertainty.
- Take hidden agendas into account by analyzing stakeholders' answers.
- Stakeholders are also important knowledge owners whom you need to convince to stay.

Steps to get you there:

1. Identify the main stakeholders related to the business process selected, as well as specific names and positions of people who represent these stakeholder groups.
2. Think carefully who might be involved, supported or even threatened by your activities, and discuss these topics with the stakeholders. Identify the gates that you need to cross in order to meet these stakeholders.
3. Decide on an appropriate form for eliciting the information required from the stakeholders. Would meeting and presentations be an appropriate form? Would individual discussions have more value?
4. Ask identified stakeholders who they think may also be stakeholders.
5. Document anticipated and preferred stakeholder opinions: current and future requirements, "ideal" requirements in terms of knowledge, and recommended actions.
6. Decide on who needs to be informed. Decide when and how communication should occur.

In order to define the opinion of the stakeholders some interviews are needed. A template of an interview guideline[16] provides the first clues.

---

[16] See subchapter Interview Guidelines

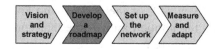

Understand the Different Types of Knowledge Needed

The identification of the required knowledge and its sources – internal and external – to support the process or task with which to ultimately achieve the business goal, is critical.

Why this is important:

- This step helps build a framework to understand what knowledge you need for the chosen business process or task.
- This unique knowledge, which could serve as a basis for obtaining or retaining a competitive advantage, should be valuable, rare, difficult to imitate and without substitutes.

Innovation

- Knowledge-sharing and creation processes serve as a basis for the innovation process. In innovation initiatives you can therefore focus on both implicit and explicit knowledge.
- Start with the coordination and re-systematization of explicit knowledge (company-internal innovation databases, reports etc.) to build a broad knowledge base. Then you can gain implicit knowledge through employees' interaction by sharing knowledge during frequent meetings.
- Besides the transfer and creation of knowledge, an increase in the transparency of the innovation process could be very useful. This could enable the firm to concentrate on strategically important knowledge and decrease redundancies (decrease costs), as well as to create synergies (increase efficiency) and minimize the risk of failures (risk minimization).

Customer Integration

- It is important to find the right customer with the right implicit knowledge. Think of questions like: Does this customer represent a specific customer group? Or should we choose him as a member because of his creative ideas (the lead user approach)?
- In building customer integration initiatives you should be mainly interested in customers' implicit knowledge. Therefore you need to ask

yourself, or the people who know this customer, whether he possesses the implicit knowledge that you need, and whether he would be willing to share it.

- Customers can also mean consumers, customer groups or companies with which you have worked. You might therefore not only ask your stakeholders what implicit knowledge is needed, but also those people who understand the business process that you want to support.

Mergers & Acquisition Integration

- Identify knowledge overlaps and lacks by comparing the knowledge bases of both firms and identifying sources of knowledge in each firm.
- Create a knowledge map of the crucial knowledge. What knowledge do you need and what knowledge do you have? It can be both implicit (individual knowledge owners) and explicit knowledge (e.g., patents or contracts).
- Knowledge is an important, and often major, incentive for decisions related to M&A, however, it is also a great challenge that only few can master. As the daily routines of the firms, which include tacit knowledge embedded in processes, undergo changes in terms of the M&A, this tacit knowledge will most probably disappear irrevocably.

 Steps to get you there:

1. Create a map of the knowledge activities by breaking down into distinct stages the process or task on which you are focused.
2. Involve yourself fully with the process and learn more about the actual mechanisms of the process or the nature of the task.
3. Talk to the relevant experts and ask their opinions on existing inefficiencies or knowledge gaps in the process or task. Many people have a good understanding of where the success or failure in such processes lies.
4. Interview people who are responsible for each stage of the business process or task.
5. Keep in mind that expert interviews will never be completely objective information sources. Experts, however, might be stakeholders as well, therefore involve some stakeholder-type question.
6. You are now able to plan the knowledge activity that is needed to speed up the process or task fulfillment.

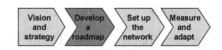

Decide on the Network Option

The purpose of this step is to determine whether a network is the most appropriate knowledge management solution with respect to the information you have collected and analyzed in the prior steps.

Why this is important:

- In order to support a specific business process, task or knowledge leverage point, you could use different organizational forms or different knowledge activities. For the success of your knowledge initiatives it is very important to not only identify the appropriate points to act on, but also to choose the appropriate form for your activity.
- It is important to answer the following questions:
    - How does the network option fit into the overall business strategy?
    - Does the company possess preconditions, e.g. routines, qualified to support a knowledge network as an organizational form?
    - What are the industry trends affecting resource allocations?
    - How do competitors deal with the knowledge network option?
- Can your goal be best reached by connecting people in an organizational form? If yes, there are different organizational forms for reaching different goals.
- Briefly summarized:
    - If you want to support the exchange of practitioners' implicit knowledge, use a community of practice option.
    - To support the exchange of implicit knowledge of people with different practical backgrounds, use a community of interest.
    - If you want to create a more formalized organizational form managed according to tasks and goals, but which is also more costly in terms of money and resources, use a knowledge network.

Innovation

- A network can help to identify innovation initiatives and help to coordinate them by means of interaction between innovation networks, as it will predefine the network characteristics and effectiveness.
- Successful network approaches can help to facilitate the creation of new network initiatives to support innovation.
- Before choosing the network option, take the following answers into consideration:
- Company structure:
  - The size of the company.
  - A centralized or decentralized company structure.
  - A formal or flat hierarchy.
  - The extent of cross-category leverage.
  - The innovations' link to the external world (e.g., suppliers/ partners/ customers).
- Innovation practice:
  - The type of innovation (product, service, process).
  - The characteristic of the central organizational driver (customer, marketing, R&D, none).
  - The extent of R&D involvement.
  - The number of functions involved in the innovation process, different functions' involvement over time.
  - Maturity of the company/division's experience with innovation.
  - Involvement of external parties in the innovation process.

Customer Integration

- To build a knowledge network with customers you need to have a strong and long-term relationship with the customers you want to integrate. A high level of trust should be developed so that the customers know the relationship has value for them and is worth developing further by working together in a network.
- Other prerequisites for choosing the network option: strong commitment by the top management, strong relationships with the customers you would choose as members, knowledge of the triggers to facilitate cooperation within the network, and transparency regarding the costs and values of the network.
- The network needs to be focused on a specific task, product or service to be able to identify the right customer and the value for the company. Decide if you want to support your customer relationship management (marketing) with the network, or if you want integrate customers'

knowledge to improve products or services, or want to create something new (customers' knowledge as a new knowledge source).

Mergers & Acquisition Integration

- The network option can't be an instrument in the first phase of the integration process, because under conditions of huge uncertainty people are not willing to share their knowledge.
- However, it is critical to consider knowledge management during all stages of an M&A process. The option of a knowledge network, or another organizational form, for the post-merger knowledge integration has to be defined on the basis of the first integration endeavors.
- Very critical factors for the overall M&A process are consistent debriefing, emphasis on communication, and speed and trust within the company. It is also important to keep record of the entire M&A process from a knowledge management perspective, and to create a database for further M&A practices.
- Take into account probable cultural differences and misunderstandings and overcome them by being trustworthy and ensuring prompt communication within the knowledge network.

 Steps to get you there:

1. Perform a SWOT analysis by comparing different organizational forms that deal with knowledge. Identify the internal strengths and weaknesses as well as the external opportunities for and threats to each form.
2. Check whether the existing types of knowledge, the given firm architecture, and culture suit the network approach in order to select the organizational form for your knowledge activities.
3. Estimate the approximate duration of the network (short term or long term).
4. Clarify the management commitment or preferences.
5. Check the resources required for each organizational alternative.

Select the Appropriate Network Reference Model

Once you have determined that building up a knowledge network is the appropriate choice for an organizational form for your planned knowledge management activities, this section will help you to select the appropriate network reference mode for the task you want to complete, and for the knowledge you need in your company.

Types of Operational Knowledge Tasks and types of Knowledge Created

The fact that the knowledge could be either explicit or implicit plays an important role, since explicit knowledge is more schematic and easier to transfer systematically than implicit knowledge, which requires a completely different approach. The network reference mode will differ according to the type of knowledge the network has to deal with and the operational knowledge task it has to fulfill. The operational knowledge task is the main knowledge process to be supported with the setting up of the network, and this can be modified or extended. For example, if the knowledge network is mainly a network of experts supporting an innovation process, the key operational knowledge task of the network could be to turn implicit knowledge into explicit knowledge by materializing it and thus making it accessible to others (see Back et al., 2005). In a narrow sense the notion of an operational knowledge task represents activities such as helping one another, consulting, benchmarking, or training.

Based on Nonaka's SECI model, there are four operational knowledge tasks from which the resulting network reference modes arises (see Nonaka and Takeuchi, 1995, p. 71):

- An *experiencing knowledge network*: combining implicit knowledge
- A *materializing knowledge network*: transforming implicit knowledge into explicit knowledge
- A *resystematizing knowledge network*: combining explicit knowledge
- A *learning knowledge network*: transforming explicit knowledge into implicit knowledge

The result of the transforming and combining processes within the particular network is new knowledge.

In an experiencing knowledge network, systematize knowledge, such as shared mental models and technical skills, prevail. On the other hand, in a materializing network, conceptual knowledge is created in the form of analogies or metaphors. In a resystematizing network, systemic knowledge, such as prototypes or new components of technologies, is created. Finally, a learning network gives rise to operational knowledge, for example, project management, production processes, or policy implementation.

The operational knowledge task describes the main task of the network that is supported by tools and the environment, but other knowledge transformation processes are also likely to take place within the network. It is therefore difficult to clearly identify the main transformation processes that need to be supported, since the boundaries are blurred. Our research has also shown that networks can change their mode over a period of time if conditions change, or the goal requires a change in the mode.[17]

 **The Learning Network of Toyota and Its Suppliers**

In practice, it is sometimes problematic to distinguish a single network reference mode. However, this example clearly describes the learning network mode, in which the members of the network learn from one member company and convert its explicit knowledge into their own implicit operational knowledge.

One of Toyota's important suppliers, the Karya-1 factory at Aisin, was completely destroyed by fire. In a highly mechanized way, this factory had produced large quantities of a small, but key, component for the brake system used in most Toyota models (as well as for cars produced by other Japanese manufacturers). As there was no second source for this component, and as these components were produced and shipped just-in-time, the impact of the disruption of the supply on Toyota's production (as on other manufacturers) was enormous. Four days later practically all Toyota's and most of its rival companies' plants were closed.

However, Toyota's powerful supplier network was literally mobilized within hours. In fact, the Aisin staff held the first meeting to consider possible solutions while the fire was still raging. It was decided that outside help was indispensable. Technical specifications were sent to the 62 companies that had offered help after receiving Aisin's call. As early as three days after the fire, one of them presented a feasible solu-

---

[17] Illustrated in the innovation network case study in this book, see chapter Supporting Growth through Innovation Networks in Unilever

tion. Others followed soon after. Following the approval of the prototypes by Aisin, various suppliers started production and subsequent shipment without a written order or legal agreement on property rights, costs etc. As dedicated equipment was lacking, the production of large numbers was difficult. Nevertheless, as a result of rapid and continuous improvement, many companies realized satisfactory increases in production levels. Consequently, Toyota's production lines re-started six days after the fire, and ten days later were once again functioning at full capacity.

The trust and commitment present within the Toyota network, as well as the competencies in collaboration and the joint technical problem solving developed within the network, allowed the network to rapidly organize the transfer of explicit information flows and convert them into the tacit knowledge required for efficient production (Nishiguchi and Beaudet, 1998).

Identify Deliverables and Choose the Appropriate Knowledge Network

A clear focus must be articulated in order to manage a *knowledge network* properly. This includes an agreement on the operative goals. You will also be able to measure the results of the network if you have defined the goals.

Why this is important:

- You have a clear focus on dealing with the most valuable resource in your company.
- Setting the proper goals initially will facilitate determining the other parameters of the network.
- Trade-offs between the company, network and individual goals must be considered.
- Trade-offs between different tasks should lead to a clear and explicit definition of the main task or to any needed adjustments.
- The link between the strategy, the business process and the goal you want to reach with the network should be totally clear to ensure that you will be able to support the growth strategy chosen.

- Keep in mind that these deliverables are still preliminary until they have been agreed on with all the network members.

Innovation

- An *innovation network* enables knowledge creation; therefore you need to go through all knowledge processes (locate/capture, share, and create) to achieve innovation.
- The network's priority could be the coordination of the innovation actions rather than constant creation of innovations. In this case the boundary setting and focusing would differ from what they would be if the network were acting as an "innovation incubator".
- The innovation network is closely connected with other organizational forms, including firms' traditional units for organizing the innovation process, project teams etc., therefore the goals and processes of these other forms should also be taken into consideration.

Customer Integration

- Customers' *knowledge integration* networks are mainly experiencing networks, which are focused on implicit knowledge sharing between customers and company employees.
- If the company has already established a strong relationship with a few key customers, there can be a *materializing network* in which customers share their knowledge and materialize their thoughts by creating guidelines for new customized service and product requirements.
- Another question that arises is the topology of the network. We have identified two main topologies that support work with customers and the integration of their knowledge.

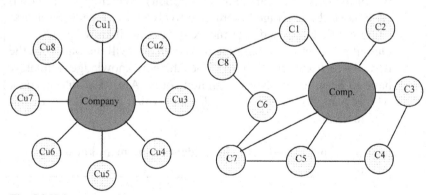

Fig. 5.2 Hub or network structure

Mergers & Acquisition Integration

- Common interest and urgencies can motivate members. In this case, knowledge integration will take place by sharing context-related knowledge.
- First concentrate on an explicit to explicit knowledge transfer, then on an explicit to implicit knowledge transfer. The transfer of implicit to implicit knowledge can be an option at an advanced stage of integration.

 Steps to get you there:

Keep in mind, that you need to identify a goal for the network that will solve a real business need in order to motivate managers to support it and members to participate in it.

1. Identify deliverables:
   The analysis in the last step, and the information collected on the process, task, or the identified knowledge leverage point will now help you to choose the appropriate knowledge activity that can most effectively support your strategic goal. In the last step, review the analysis to make a more educated choice.

2. Identify the knowledge and choose the appropriate knowledge activity:
   In order to identify your operational knowledge task, consider the following questions from two different perspectives:
   Input perspective: What is the prevalent type of knowledge with which the network deals (explicit/implicit)? Which type of knowledge has to be leveraged more effectively and efficiently – the existing implicit knowledge or the existing explicit knowledge?
   Output perspective: What type of knowledge will the output of the network be (explicit/implicit)? Does the new knowledge ultimately have to be in an explicit or implicit form? Also take into account who is going to use the knowledge and which output is most valuable to them.

The answers from (1) and (2) help to identify the main knowledge operational task.

Set Up the Selected Network Type

Once the set-up has been planned, you then have to establish the knowledge network. The following section includes all the steps necessary to build up a knowledge network for growth: from the identification of specific network goals and tasks to the development of a communication plan, the composition of a management board and factors to facilitate management commitment. Facilitating the relationships within the network will be discussed as well as organizing the people and meetings. External relationships with other networks and company processes allowing the proliferation of the network's work throughout the company will also be explained.

The aim of this step is to promote the set-up process, i.e. to map the business area or process within your company that you want to support with a knowledge network and pointers on how to facilitate management support.

Identify Your Specific Goals, Tasks and Activities

At this stage it is important to keep the results of the previous step *select a process or task* in mind, since you have to implement the results of the step that identified the main operational task. The main issue of the present step is to identify the company's needs, and to derive the goals for the knowledge network. This is the spadework for the following step of top management facilitation and the development of the knowledge board.

Furthermore, the goals of the knowledge network indicate the tasks to be solved by the knowledge network members. The tasks can be divided into tasks with a short-term and long-term perspective. It seems reasonable to first concentrate on the tasks with a short-term perspective in order to provide early successes. Such "quick win" actions will demonstrate the work of this new organizational form and ensure its business entitlement. In the following, a sensible composition of tasks with short-term and long-term perspectives ensures the continuity and the strategic scope of the knowledge network.

Why this is important:

- The quantification and operationalization of goals serve to facilitate management commitment, as it makes the knowledge network more tangible.
- The goals determine the competencies and skills needed in the knowledge network.
- The affiliation of the participants with the knowledge network is primarily task-related.
- This step is key in quantifying and operationalizing the knowledge gaps in order to later implement the performance measurement.

Innovation

- You have to keep in mind that the goal of this type of knowledge network ought to align all the innovation projects.
- In order to map the goals, tasks and activities, you have to undertake several investigations in order to determine the goals and tasks of the knowledge network. In the beginning, you need an overview of the current innovation projects related to the same research fields. Thereafter, you have to prioritize the current projects in order to compare the current situation with the expected situation. Based on the last step, you may find gaps between the two and thus be able to pinpoint future projects. The gaps are an innovation network's field of activity.

Customer Integration

- In order to gain the full potential of the knowledge network, you have to identify a business need within your company that can only be solved by a customer network. The stakeholders can help to identify the purpose of the network and its related tasks.
- A customer is not an employee; the customer is a voluntary participant in the knowledge network. You thus need to find an appropriate balance between the company's business needs and the creation of value for the customers. In order to identify the potential tasks to be solved by the customers and the company, you have to discuss these tasks on the basis of the management proposal.
- Customers provide the best feedback. You can discuss the possible tasks to be solved in the network's kick-off meeting and together with the customers decide which goals you all want to reach and which task they find both interesting and valuable.

- Despite the intellectual property rights issue, you have to build trust among the knowledge network participants; you have ensure that there is transparency regarding the company's aims for the network and the customers' individual agendas. Both are crucial for a well functioning knowledge network, as hidden agendas are a counterproductive factor in a network.

Mergers & Acquisition Integration

- Before the merger or acquisition, both companies obviously had different approaches to the same procedures. You therefore have to focus on understanding the procedures in both companies in order to understand their differences, synergies, and common issues.
- Once the procedures in both companies have been identified, you have to compare them in order to find the best practices in each. The sharing of best practices can serve as a task to be solved.
- A further means to map your field of activity is through the comparison of the actual integration approaches and the strategic direction of the company in which the integration gaps appear. To prevent conflict with other integration measures, you have to take them into account and compare them with yours.
- The potential tasks ought to be discussed in a meeting between the top management and the members.

 Steps to get you there:

1. Conduct interviews with the people involved in the processes.
2. Familiarize yourself with the processes you need in order to fill the knowledge gaps.
3. Identify the goals of the knowledge network.
4. Specify what skills and competencies are needed to fulfill each of the knowledge network's goals.
5. In order to obtain the top management's commitment, submit a list of the goals and the human resources required to the top management and let them decide on the primary goals and the human resources that they are willing to supply.
6. Make your goals, tasks and activities articulate and visible through benchmarking and measuring.
7. An agreement on the tasks to be solved is a mutual decision by all the knowledge network participants, it is therefore advisable to

> prepare a set of tasks. During the kick-off workshop let the partici-
> pants decide on the primary tasks to be solved in order to guaran-
> tee a common understanding.

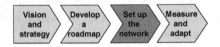

Composition of the Knowledge Board

The knowledge board is a group of people who support the knowledge network and help assess its knowledge. The purpose of the knowledge board is to give strategic direction in order to provide the focus and the level of investment in knowledge management and network-development activities, and to provide influence when and where needed to ensure the effectiveness of these investments. They should, furthermore, connect the network tasks with the functional lines.

Why this is important:

- The purpose of the knowledge board is to give strategic direction, provide focus and a level of investment in knowledge and network-development activities, and to intervene when and where needed, in order to ensure the effectiveness of these investments.
- The knowledge board helps the knowledge management department keep knowledge management initiatives feasible, focused, and appropriately funded, by knowing what is going on and by sanctioning the knowledge management department to coordinate knowledge management efforts throughout the entire company.

Innovation

- A knowledge board of innovation directors might support the communication with other business units as well as ensure the top management's commitment.
- If your innovation network consists of middle management representatives, it is doubtful whether a knowledge board would be beneficial. Middle managers usually have enough power to promote the network and gain financial resources themselves.

Customer Integration

- The knowledge board of a customer network will primarily consist of representatives from your company, but also from customers' firms. Both sides may communicate the obtained results to their companies, thereby enhancing the knowledge network commitment.
- It is important to develop a good communication strategy for contact with the customers' management, and to provide their management with the values to be gained from their involvement, and with the reasons for choosing them as a member. Also clarify the values for your company as well as providing the names of some potential network members to ensure support. It is important to point out the investments in time and resources that are necessary to ensure success.

Mergers & Acquisition Integration

- Sometimes, not the all business units in a company are affected by an M&A. A knowledge board should therefore only consists of the managers who are directly involved. This combination of people guarantees that the knowledge network will perform well and that the assigned resources will be appropriate and sufficient, since the board members all have a personal interest in the success of the integration.

 Steps to get you there:

1. The knowledge board can be a crucial instrument with which to link network activities with the matrix organization as well as an instrument through which to communicate. It serves as an internal marketing instrument as well as a communication platform for the knowledge management's activities.
2. Provide the knowledge board with concrete ideas for support and for the required resources.
3. Conduct formal interviews as well as informal networking to understand senior management's interests and priorities, to educate them about knowledge management elements and strategies, and to identify appropriate members for an effective knowledge board.
4. In order to match the requirements of the knowledge board, take the following questions and hints into account:
   - Define how the knowledge network can gain value to reach

company goals.
- What does the knowledge board expect such a network to do?
- What are the costs and what are the benefits?
- Which resources are appropriate?
- How often do they need to be informed?
- How can you ensure that the knowledge board's communication is extended to their business unit or functional lines?

Justification Process and Communication Plan

The justification process and the communication plan depict the first information collected on the goals, tasks and deliverables of the knowledge network. They are aimed at revealing the feasibility of the network to the management in order to obtain their acceptance of and support for the knowledge network. The justification process and communication plan are a preparatory step for the composition of the knowledge board and the facilitation of the top management commitment that will follow.

Why this is important:

- The identified needs ought to be consolidated in an understandable form and be given to the relevant people.
- A knowledge network requires a significant investment to justify this investment and its results should add significant value to the business.
- In order to obtain financial and human resources, the management ought to see tangible benefits emanate from the knowledge network.

Innovation

- Innovation is aligned with the company's strategy therefore you should ensure that the communication plan is aligned with the company's vision and strategy.
- Build communication by linking the network with existing innovation and network activities in the firm by using existing routines.

- Ensure regional and global communication to create transparency and management buy-in of the innovation activities. A network can help to create this transparency as well as to find gaps.

Customer Integration

- Make sure that all stakeholders within the company have agreed to the network, its purpose and the costs of integrating customers. Once the customer knowledge network is running, it will be detrimental to the company to terminate it, as this will convey an incorrect impression of customer value to the stakeholders. Stakeholders will gain a similar negative impression if the company were to terminate a customer knowledge network as a result of its costs. The premature and sudden termination of a customer knowledge network could also destroy the trust in the company. A carefully planned and widely communicated internal initiative is thus a success factor in keeping a knowledge network alive and will furthermore ensure customers' loyalty.
- As customers are a company's most valuable assets, reflect carefully on your communication with them. Think of the appropriate media to use to keep them informed and find the appropriate person for the communication. One possible means of communication is to use a member of the top management, since this conveys to customers that the company values them.
- Successful initiatives, such as customer knowledge networks, have a huge marketing potential as they reveal the company's customer-centric strategy. Before advertising the customer knowledge network, first ensure that the endeavor is a success for both parties.
- Unfortunately, not all of a company's customers can participate in a knowledge network. It is therefore necessary to also consider the counterproductive effects of having to communicating with customers who are not future members of the network.

Mergers & Acquisition Integration

- A merger or an acquisition entails a reorganization of the company. You have to take into account that as a result of the merger the employees might be tired of changes and reorganization procedures, therefore you ought to communicate the knowledge network as an amelioration of the daily business.
- The justification process and communication plan should include and reveal the lacking knowledge and knowledge gaps due to the merger.

- You have to take the needs of your target group into account. The management may want to see increased profit generated by the knowledge network, but the employees want to see job security.

Steps to get you there:

1. Define the key mission, values and benefits of the knowledge network as based on the stakeholder analysis and the identified specific goals, tasks and activities.
2. Make sure that the knowledge vision and values are in line with the company's mission and values.
3. Clarify the tasks of the network, perform benchmark studies and prioritize the tasks according to the time schedule.
4. Develop a communication strategy for
   - Top management by means of a business plan
   - The individual or potential members by means of presentations.
5. Give thought to how you would communicate failures.
6. Each member reports back to his own organization or business unit. Provide each member with material required for communication and assign the material to an individual member.
7. Involve the initiator of the knowledge network in communication. Story telling is often a more effective method of gaining senior management's commitment.
8. Adapt your justification process and communication strategy to the target group.

An outline of the communication process is to be found in the template section.[18]

Facilitate Top Management Commitment and Find Sponsors

The initialization of a knowledge network and its further development is facilitated by top management commitment, since they can provide financial and human resources. This commitment can set an example for the participants and also has the effect of justifying the knowledge network.

---

[18] See subchapter Outline of Communication

Why this is important:

- Some senior managers are convinced by the fit of the network goals with their individual vision, and therefore qualitative objectives.
- Middle management tends to be easier convinced by figures than by qualitative objectives. Therefore try to provide an example of the cost savings and additional margins that a knowledge network could provide.
- When an organization attempts to establish a knowledge network, members are more likely to invest time and effort if the network has the full and convincing support of the top management, since top management sets an example.
- If you have to deal with members who are hard to convince, try to visualize the cause-and-effect relationship of the network in the company. Complexity theory provides a tool called method visualizing to indicate such a cause and effect (for further details, see the step *measure and adapt*).

Innovation

- Innovation is a strategic theme; therefore you ought to find sponsors in the technology, R&D and marketing departments to facilitate the initialization of an innovation network. This can best be done by providing the management with a performance measurement, e.g. if you work for a global company, the performance measurement might be a decrease in redundancy in the innovation projects.
- To measure the network's performance, you could quantify the extrapolated results in two sequential steps. First, monitor the network progress by measuring the number of innovation projects per region, country, and on a global level, measuring the number of projects in each phase of the innovation project development funnel, such as idea generation, launch preparation, production, follow-up and, finally, reveal the free resources to contributed to added value. Second, estimate the network's added value by counting the number of innovation rollouts, and the total number of redundant projects.

Customer Integration

- The top management's commitment to the knowledge network is essential to provide resources and sponsorship for the knowledge network. The management needs to see the value of the network, e.g., better core customer loyalty, but also the risks, such as losing customers' loyalty if the knowledge network fails.

- Establishing awareness is very important, especially in the customer's company, since this company's employees have to know that their participation in the knowledge network is appreciated. The customer needs to see high hierarchical-level support, i.e. management involvement indicates that the company feels that its customers are important. It is thus imperative to integrate top management in all communication with customers and in the kick-off event to demonstrate the attention paid to them.
- When searching for an appropriate sponsor within your company, ensure that you also find sponsors in the customers' companies to support their involvement by explaining the value it may have for their own company.

Mergers & Acquisition Integration

- The appropriate time for an M&A integration network is after the technical and organizational integration. You have to take into account that the management might have a different opinion of the post-merger integration than the operational layer does, i.e. they might consider the post-merger integration a closed affair. It is therefore necessary to find sponsors on a higher hierarchical level who are directly involved in the post-merger integration and show them the strategic challenges that ought to be overcome by the M&A integration network, and involve top management from both former companies.
- The employees' awareness of the barriers to overcome is pivotal. Create an awareness of the network by presenting the M&A integration network as a continuation of the technical and operational integration measures.

 Steps to get you there:

1. Discuss what should be measured with the top management and visualize the cause and effect of network interaction.
2. Previous successful examples of knowledge initiatives can support the awareness and importance of the resource "knowledge" and the necessity of dealing with this resource.

3. Examples, e.g., cases of similar solutions in different companies, have a positive effect on the management's decision, since the examples illustrate the value of a knowledge network quite plainly.
4. Show and explain the resources needed. A business plan might help to find sponsors (see the case beneath).
5. Identify individual vision of key stakeholders, and show the fit of the network with their visions.

A Utility Company's Business Plan for Top Management

A template[19] offers a possible structure and outline of a business plan. In addition, a structure and argumentation of a presentation is offered as a template[20].

 **RWE Net**

An RWE Net knowledge network leader had to gain management support. He needed personal resources to initialize a knowledge network. One of the obstacles, however, was that the employees' workload was very high due to the reorganization of the company. In addition, the management was reluctant to release personnel resources.

The knowledge network leader persuaded the management that a knowledge network was needed in order to formalize the transfer of knowledge, which had not been considered by other approaches that supported the integration of geographically dispersed employees. The commitment of the management for the initiative was to be gained through feasible outcomes and hard figures.

He used a business plan to gain his top management's commitment. The business plan also served as a basis for the management's decision as well as a guide to decision making for the knowledge network. The business plan demonstrated the opportunities and risks associated with a knowledge network, and made the knowledge network transparent to the management.

---

[19] See subchapter The Business Plan
[20] See subchapter Presentations to Convince Management

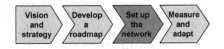

Facilitate the Relationships within the Network

Since you have to deal with implicit knowledge, you have to persuade the appropriate people to become members of a network and establish a relationship among them. As a first step in this section, we have to facilitate the commitment of the potential members. Secondly, the different roles specifically defined for a particular network have to be identified according to the skills needed. Thirdly, meetings have to be organized. The last two steps in this section demonstrate how organizational tools and ICT tools can help support the members of a knowledge network.

Facilitate Members' Commitment

Before you can initialize a network, you ought to gain the members' commitment, because people are the most important part of a knowledge network. The network members' commitment to the network is fundamental for its smooth cooperation.

Why this is important:

- Without the commitment of all the knowledge network participants, the group will not work as a group and the network will not perform better than a single member could.

Innovation

- Despite their voluntary participation in a knowledge network, the commitment of knowledge network members should be stimulated through top management support of the initiative. Top management, in turn, should be motivated by the lessening of redundancies in some business units as result of the network activities.
- Tacit knowledge is the most important source of innovation. Because tacit knowledge is related to people, factors that enable its sharing and creation have to be implemented through activities such as an innovation network. The network members' commitment could be enhanced by an indication of the potential value of a knowledge network, like lessons learned, and getting to know other innovation endeavors.

Customer Integration

- All the members come from different cultures; they have a different organizational background and have different mentalities, or even hidden agendas. These aspects can build barriers between the knowledge network participants. Only trust and care within the network can overcome these barriers and create the openness needed for knowledge sharing.
- Trust is an important factor in this network, and it facilitates the members' commitment. Despite the question of intellectual property rights, we should build openness within the network.
- Success factors for establishing an appropriate atmosphere within the network:
  - Building openness and trust.
  - Consistent monitoring, updating and testing of the customer knowledge flowing into the network to support the building of trust between the customers and the company.
  - Motivating people by establishing a win-win situation.

Mergers & Acquisition Integration

- A merger or an acquisition inevitably entails a reorganization of the whole company. Furthermore, the involved companies are never free of redundancies of people's experiences. Various barriers that might hinder the cooperation between people and the knowledge network might therefore occur.
  - The employees might be tired of changes after the reorganization.
  - The experienced internal competition might hinder the transfer of knowledge and thus, the initialization of a knowledge network.
  - People might fear losing their position, since the reorganization aims on eliminating redundancies.
- It is therefore important to explain that a knowledge network is not simply another reorganization, but provides long-term stability.
- Explain the possible values to be gained to the participants.

 Steps to get you there:

1. Not all participants cooperate altruistically with other people. You have to keep in mind that some knowledge network members need to see a clear personal value that can be derived from the work within the knowledge network.

---

2. The personal value may be, e.g., members' recognition as experts by their co-workers or their management and a better performance in their daily work, which might result in their advancement within their companies.
3. Question the potential participants on their acceptance of a knowledge network initiative, and act proactively.
4. The not-invented-here syndrome can be one of the major barriers in the company. The selection of appropriate goals and tasks for the knowledge network is one means to overcome this barrier.

Interviews provide the means to obtain insights into members' feelings and affiliations; you can use the interview guideline template as a starting point.[21]

Determine the Roles and Responsibilities

Although a knowledge network tends to be self-regulated by the participants, it needs a rudimentary structure. The rudimentary structure prevents anyone having a free ride and it gives the participants a structure in which they know what to expect and how to act.

Why this is important:

- One of the structural conditions for successful group work is the clear and explicit determination of roles and responsibilities. Furthermore, the roles and responsibilities in the knowledge network form a minimal structure within the network.
- Unclear structures and duties tend to hinder the work of a group, since nobody then accepts responsibility for work such as the preparation of meetings, and the moderation of workshops etc. Roles and responsibilities therefore give a knowledge network transparency.
- The participants' roles and responsibilities depend on their experience and affiliation with a knowledge network. However, the roles and responsibilities are not fixed and they can change over the years.

---

[21] See subchapter Interview Guidelines

- Sometimes people tend to feel discriminated against, especially when they feel they are doing more than what is required. To provide transparency in the knowledge network structure, it is useful to list the responsibilities, the related tasks and targets, and to discuss these with each member or potential member.

The following section describe the key roles of each knowledge network for growth.

Innovation

- Besides the importance of all roles in a network, two key roles have to be established in a innovation network:
  - The sponsors of a knowledge network have to come from senior management, because innovation is a strategic issue.
  - The active members of an innovation network should be R&D representatives.

Customer Integration

- The network leader is crucial for a customer network, for he has to represent both company participants and customers. He ensures that the network operations are controlled, and communicates the activities within the knowledge network to the outside world.
- He knows how gain the required knowledge from customers.
- He should be a company employee, as this facilitates the network's utilization of company resources and ensures the transfer of knowledge to the rest of the company.

Mergers & Acquisition Integration

- The first role to be identified is the role of an M&A integration network leader. It is a primary role within an M&A integration network. He organizes, coordinates and integrates the network activities, and generally facilitates the work within the network, the knowledge transfer, and the integration. A network leader has to be a neutral person, in the sense that he is acceptable to all the company employees. He has to know how to treat the employees from the previous companies, and how to motivate the network members.
- In some cases it is reasonable to have two network leader in the start-up phase of the M&A network, one from each former company, to ensure

that the initiative is not perceived as being imposed by one of the former companies on the other.

- The persons who have the best overview of the post-merger integration are the integration managers. They can provide their insights into the post-merger integration and coordinate with other integration initiatives. It is therefore reasonable to involve the integration manager in the M&A integration network.

 Steps to get you there:

Besides the above-emphasized roles, a knowledge network requires further roles and responsibilities. The determination of roles and responsibilities depends on persons' skills, experience and their hierarchical position. There are four roles with their corresponding responsibilities.

Sponsors are from top management. They provide the knowledge network with financial and human resources. They furthermore govern the knowledge network.

The network leader has the most pivotal role. He might come from various hierarchical levels. The selection criteria in this case are his experience with the knowledge network issues as well as his abilities, such as social skills, moderation and presentation skills. His responsibilities are the initialization and the maintenance of the knowledge network. He is thus responsible for the identification of the members, and coordinating and organizing the work and the meetings.

Members constitute the knowledge network. They are the key players in the network. The can be differentiated according to their experience in the network, i.e. they can be novices or more experienced members. They are only appropriate members of a knowledge network if they are interested in the specific knowledge topic and can gain personal benefit from solving the task. The members are responsible for solving individual tasks that are necessary to reach the proposed goals.

External experts are temporary participants in a knowledge network. Their experience is required when the members are not able to perform a specific task, e.g., the implementation of ICT tools requires a deeper understanding of IT issues.

Organize the People and the Meetings

The exchange of tacit knowledge requires a close interaction and communication between the members of a network. Despite the use of ICT tools, face-to-face meetings provide the best means with which to create social ties among knowledge network members. It is especially during the initiation of a knowledge network that such meetings give the members a sense of belonging. Needless to say, the subsequent face-to-face meetings are significant for the performance of the knowledge network.

Why this is important:

- Regular meetings give the group a sense of belonging that will have a positive impact on the trust building process. Additionally, regular meetings guarantee that the visibility of a knowledge network is maintained.
- The formalized approach of a knowledge network requires a clear starting point. A kick-off workshop, in which all the participants may meet one another, facilitates the trust-building process among the members.
- The sharing of unstructured experiences among the knowledge network participants is facilitated by face-to-face communication.
- Workshops help members learn through one another's experiences and allow discussions that build strong relationships and help to improve capabilities.
- This helps members to accelerate their own professional development and to obtain new insights and methods that can be applied to solve particular problems.
- Often workshops have to be used to integrate the members in the network concept by deducing what they find motivating and which other people need to be integrated as well.

Innovation

- Besides people's experience or position within the company, a common ground is needed before they can be network members. The possible participants ought to show an interest in obtaining the big picture regarding the innovation situation in the company as well as indicating an interest in the mutual sharing of new ideas and practices.
- Although innovation is the work field of R&D personnel, you have to have an open mind about other areas. There is an option to link the network with the external environment through the inclusion of external participants, like marketing or sales personnel.
- Very often, informal networks are found in a company. You can use previous experience of informal structures in order to enhance the building of a formal structure.
- The daily communication is organized via e-mail and, if available, company-wide innovation systems.

Customer Integration

- In the inter-organizational knowledge network, the members are the most crucial factor. Thus, only customers experienced with your products or services will create value for your company. The company representatives ought to be carefully selected. They ought to possess enough experience to provide value for the customers. On the other hand, only appropriate company representatives can ensure knowledge sharing on a high level and can transfer the knowledge back into other departments (e.g., Marketing, Product Development or Support).
- The cooperation between the knowledge network members is based on face-to-face meetings and virtual cooperation. The main work will be done in virtual meetings because the customers are geographically separated, and participate under time constrains. In order to facilitate the work of the network, ICT tools, which support the virtual communication and cooperation between the members, are a key success factor.
- The period between the face-to-face meetings will not be constant, because this will depend on the task to be solved and the time constrains of the participants.
- Keeping the same participants in the knowledge network provides a good opportunity to build trust. Nevertheless, it is possible to integrate external sources if a task requires people with other experience who are not as yet involved in the knowledge network.
- The identification of the knowledge network members might take some time, because we have to identify them according to their interaction

with the company. The channel by which appropriate customers can be identified, leads through the marketing or support department as well as through customer interviews, and feedback from customers after activities or events.

Mergers & Acquisition Integration

- The post-merger integration may lead to reluctance on the part of employees to cooperate with one another due to the competition among employees and due to their fear of losing their jobs. Meetings should provide an appropriate atmosphere in which network members can easily share their knowledge and in which the integration of employees is enabled. The appropriate atmosphere consists of a reciprocal understanding of one another, the willingness and capacity of employees to transfer and receive capabilities, and discretionary resources.
- During the meetings, you have to cope with two relevant issues concerning an M&A integration network. Firstly, you have to deal with the integration of the employees from two formerly different companies. You have to overcome the existing barriers between them, such as distrust, different languages and different social systems. Secondly and simultaneously, you have to keep the knowledge network running smoothly in order to provide a means for problem-solving cooperation.
- A further means of integration is the conjoint preparation of meetings. Knowledge network members from different locations have to be placed together to help the network leader prepare and organize the face-to-face meetings. The joint preparation enables the members to get to know other members from other locations better and this creates a sense of responsibility for the meeting.
- You have to find the right balance between a governed knowledge network and a self-directed knowledge network. If the management emphasizes a specific field of activity you have to manage the knowledge network. If the members have relevant issues, let them perform the tasks themselves.

 Steps to get you there:

1. In order to enhance a constructive kick-off workshop, you have to prepare it properly. It is an event with a duration from one to several days in which you convene a group of potential network participants to start developing the knowledge network.

2. The kick-off workshop should serve as an information and working event.
3. The choice of participants for the kick-off workshop has to be based on the experience needed. However, you have to ensure that they have a common interest, therefore you have to explore their willingness to participate beforehand.
4. You have to give the kick-off workshop participants enough opportunity to concretize their ideas during the workshop, but simultaneously you have to align the group work with the predetermined goals of the knowledge network.
5. The kick-off workshop is the initial starting point of the knowledge network. The following face-to-face meetings build on the results gained from the kick off workshop.
6. As participation in a knowledge network is voluntary, the meetings ought to have value for the participants. The generic three-part approach of the meetings is:
   - An orientation aiming at aligning the participants and communicating the goals of the meeting.
   - The working session in which the participants share knowledge, collect ideas, assess ideas, and work.
   - The closure aimed at defining the measures and deliverables in terms of human resources, time, kind of work, and the place of the deliverables.
7. Find a balance between self-direction and governance of the network. Therefore ask the participants what important task they want to perform as a network, while they also have to keep in mind that the management has already identified the crucial business needs that the network should support.
8. Take the team-building cycle, which ought to be fully implemented, into consideration. The first phase is the warming up of the people through the introduction of the topics, so that the participants can approve the topics. However, the following storming phase could disturb the pleasant atmosphere, since some participants might have hidden agendas and there could be concealed conflicts. The last phases are the norming and performing phases in which most of the disagreement ought to disappear by discovering common issues and all members finally agree to the topics and are aligned.
9. During the kick-off workshop, the focus should be both on content (expertise) as well as on process, i.e. how are people going to work together, and why in the form of a knowledge network).
10. The frequency of network meetings should be discussed and

agreed on in the kick-off workshop. Throughout the lifecycle of the network the frequency of meetings can change depending on the urgency of the tasks to be carried out. Two meetings per year should be the recommended minimum.

 HP's Customer Network Kick off

In order to carry out the strategic approach of a customer-centric company, HP launched a customer network, which ought to ameliorate its customer relationships and provide the company with helpful insights into its own products and services. The official starting point of the knowledge network was a kick-off meeting in which all participants met each other for the first time. The kick-off had a three-part build-up: introduction, working session and completion (see also the appendix for the detailed kick-off approach). The main purpose of the kick-off meeting was to find the tasks that both its customers and HP find motivating and valuable and to create awareness of the network among all participants.

The agenda of the kick-off workshop was thus drawn up to first provide an introduction to the topic of a knowledge network and to the concept of a customer network. The introduction should deliver awareness of the customer network. The top management's presence and involvement emphasized the importance of a customer network.

The presentation of the customer network concept accentuated that the customers' help and involvement were needed, since only through their contribution could the network be adapted to the required needs of all the participants. An indicative set of tasks to be solved by the network participants served as basic discussion points for the following working session. The aim of this part of the kick-off workshop was to deal with the open points and especially the question of motivation and the appropriate task.

The final part of the kick-off workshop completed the work done during the course of the day and acted as the final drive to motivate the customers for a customer network. The concrete tasks were identified during the last part so that the participants might leave the workshop with an idea for a concrete task. They could then communicate their ideas within their company to motivate the stakeholders within their companies.

A template of a kick-off workshop is provided later in the book [22].

Organize the Specific Processes

The specific process is the coordination of the work in the knowledge network. This serves to link the company and knowledge network's knowledge processes (locate/capture, transfer/share and create) with the business process to ensure that knowledge is created from the very beginning and that it adds value to the selected business processes and business goals. This step is aimed at organizing the processes that are needed to provide this link as well as the knowledge processes that should take place in the knowledge network.

Why this is important:

- The justification of the knowledge network depends on the performance of the work done. An early organization of the link provides a smooth transition of the network's work to the organization.

Innovation

- The first of the specific processes in the innovation is the creativity process. For all innovation projects a company needs various perspectives of as well as creativity processes for the challenge to be solved. The following steps indicate the creativity and supporting processes.
  - Deep-dive: You ought to understand and visualize the challenge of the product or service you want to improve. Observation of the use or components of the product and services provides a useful hint to facilitate understanding.
  - Total immersion into the product: Once you have understood the challenge of the product or service, you ought to find possible solutions. The best way is through the use of brainstorming.
  - Evaluation: The obtained results of the brainstorming phase ought to be evaluated in order to focus the solutions.

---

[22] See subchapter Kick-off Workshop

- Redo the deep-dive: The last step should match the found solution with the customer's requirements.

Customer Integration

- It seems to be clear that the aim of such an extended knowledge network is the solution of relevant and mutually urgent tasks. A common task provides a basis for smooth co-operation between heterogeneous members of the knowledge network and customers. To fulfill the goals detailed in the given tasks, the processes need to be organized very professionally by the network leader.
- Besides that, a clear description and discussion of the process within the network will support the virtual work of its members. Because the customers are not part of the company and cannot often meet, the working processes need to be organized by means of face-to-face meetings. In between these meetings, opportunities for virtual cooperation should be provided to offer the customers more interaction.
- The process should be in line with the members' working processes so as to support their daily work and should not be counterproductive.

Mergers & Acquisition Integration

- The M&A integration network is usually not the only means with which to integrate the company after the merger and acquisition. There are various integration approaches that may be followed during the post-merger phase. In order to gain synergies, take these other integration approaches that your company may be implementing into account by involving the integration mangers in your network initiative.
- During a first meeting with them, you should discuss and visualize the ongoing integration projects in their field of experience. This facilitates the creation of awareness of the integration gaps and overlaps among the meeting's participants. The creation of awareness furthermore facilitates the spotting of possible gaps in the integration fields as well as making everyone aware of the projects done in the former separate entities.
- The identified gaps in integration fields are the tasks that need to be done by the network. You have to focus on an integration gap that is related to the strategic orientation of the company.

Steps to get you there:

1. In order to link the tasks of the knowledge network with the business processes, you should consider having interfaces between the network tasks and the business processes.
2. The participants involved in the knowledge network should specify the business processes and their position within the company, which forms the interface.

Provide Organizational Tools to Enhance Knowledge Sharing and Knowledge Absorption

Organizational tools are a set of techniques, or methods or procedures applied to and during the meetings. Their aim is to develop a common understanding among the network participants and develop unity.

Why this is important:

- Effective knowledge sharing and creation best occur in a knowledge-enriching environment where openness, one's own initiative, and the freedom to articulate one's opinion are acceptable.

Innovation

- In multi-unit companies, personnel transfer is a very efficient organizational tool in the pre-competitive phases of the R&D process. The practice of exchanging researchers or sending scientists abroad is an excellent source of new ideas and fosters creativity in all the relevant network participants.
- Creativity is critical in the first phase of the innovation process. The practice of exchanging researchers or sending scientists abroad will deliver the same results as in the above point.
- A gatekeeper is a person who establishes informal and formal networks with his (team's) environment, such as other business units, other project teams and the company's external knowledge resources (Allen, 1977). Early work on innovation management indicated that innovation teams benefited from having a gatekeeper on the team. He scans and interprets the team's environment and then passes on the information to the team (Allen, 1977; Katz and Tushman, 1979). You should therefore

establish gatekeeper meetings in order to enhance creativity and innovation performance.

Customer Integration

- Organizational tools are important for the transfer of implicit knowledge, which is the main knowledge-related task of the network. Although this is best done through face-to-face communication, it becomes complicated if customers are geographically distant from the network center. Virtual communication through information and communication tools could thus possibly play a dominant role.
- Depending on the tasks, tools like knowledge forums, think tanks, workshops, knowledge units, coffee corners, meetings, presentations and organizational development tools can be an effective way of achieving results. These tools, chosen in the correct combination and professionally realized, can produce additional motivation, for example, through an attractive meeting place, good food, a friendly atmosphere and an overall feeling of a firm caring about its customers.
- It is not obvious which tools will be effective during which of the new network's stages. The challenge faced by a network lie in introducing the important issues to the customers, and letting the network and/or the network leader find their own way of acting by creating their own organizational culture. This culture will not equal either the firm's culture, nor to the customer's company culture. We assume that it will be an individual – and not yet defined – social interaction, way of behavior and environment.
- Organizational tools, through the initiating of personal relationships, face-to-face contacts, and geographical and social proximity, create an important atmosphere of trust inside the network. Nevertheless, the customers cannot spend as much time as the firm's own employees on mutual meetings and programs. To this end a balance between organizational and ICT tools has to be found and this is a subtle and crucial decision that has to be taken within the network.

Mergers & Acquisition Integration

- As an organizational tool, a kick-off workshop is the initial point of the M&A integration network during which we can start to overcome the personal barriers between employees, such as prejudices and language differences.

- The organizational tools ought to establish an appropriate atmosphere to overcome barriers. The first kick-off workshop should therefore take place in a neutral place, away from the daily business.
- In the initial phase of an M&A integration network, face-to-face meetings play a significant role in establishing unity between the participants. Well-prepared face-to-face meetings are crucial, since only a direct interaction with the other employees enhance the chances of eliminating prejudices.
- Real knowledge integration can only take place when real cooperation and interaction are occurring. It is therefore more important to have working group sessions and to conduct discussion than listening to monologues and presentations during face-to-face meetings.

Steps to get you there:

1. Although the culture has a relevant impact on the behavior of the knowledge network participants, you can proactively influence the knowledge-enriching environment by using tools to influence the environment. The influence on the environment can be indirect, like establishing trust, or direct, like indicating knowledge gaps. You can therefore create a micro-environment within the knowledge network.

2. The predominant goal of participation in the knowledge network is the transfer and recording of not explicated and unstructured knowledge. During their participation in the knowledge network, the participants reveal their experience and working procedures, which would not have been transferred during the usual working routines.

3. As the knowledge network participants possess unstructured and not explicated knowledge, you have to externalize and visualize the experiences of the participants during the first face-to-face meeting. The externalization and visualization will enable you to find the appropriate field of discussion, challenges as well as best practices, which will lead to an exchange of implicit knowledge.

4. For these purposes, you have to select the appropriate organizational tools with which to provide the expected result of knowledge exchange, e.g., half-day meetings with agendas explicitly focusing on the exchange of experience in a specific field.

5. For this purpose, presentations, storytelling and working group sessions are appropriate means. Keep in mind that the externalized experiences have to be recorded during meetings, since the externalization ought to build a common knowledge base for all the participants.

6. Organizational tools create an important atmosphere of trust inside the network. Meetings in a pleasant room and in an agreeable place can be seen as supportive factors, as are additional events like evening events or factory visits. Do not underestimate a good dinner either.

7. The various organizational tools can be applied, depending on the specific life cycle of the knowledge network, since each phase of the life cycle requires different organizational tools. A further issue pertaining to organizational tools is their relevance to the main activities undertaken by the knowledge network partici-

pants.
8. In the initial phase of a knowledge network, you have to empha-size that all the participants are members of the network and pro-vide them with a clearly defined starting point. The members ought to recognize the other participants' experiences and get in touch with one another. The participants also need an explanation of the knowledge network concept.
9. Initial phase: Kick-off workshop:
10. Organizational tools:
   - Presentation aimed at delivering the idea of the knowledge network concept.
   - Working group sessions with the focus on participants' knowledge identification.
   - Establishment of rules and responsibilities.
11. During later phases of the network life cycle, the emphasis lies on the main activities of the knowledge network. Each of the main activities requires different organizational tools.
12. Regularly held meetings ought to concentrate on the field of ac-tion and challenges to be solved. Organizational tools, like mod-erated workshops and presentations, enhance the finding of so-lutions to the challenges and field of action.
13. Organizational tools:
   - In an *experiencing* and *materializing knowledge network*, the focus is on communication and direct interaction, since the members have to share implicit knowledge. Organizational tools that can be potentially used during the transfer of im-plicit knowledge are: workshops, coffee corners and talk rooms, and working group sessions.
   - In a *resystematizing knowledge network*, the knowledge net-work participants have to deal with explicit knowledge. The systematization and presentation of knowledge are key. Pres-entation techniques and retrieval systems provide the means.
   - In a *learning knowledge network*, the organizational tools ought to enhance the transformation of explicit knowledge into implicit knowledge. A combination of the earlier-mentioned organizational tools delivers the appropriate in-struments.

Organize the Appropriate ICT Architecture

Besides the face-to-face meetings, ICT tools too are aimed at the transfer of explicit knowledge. ICT tools can help to overcome geographical distances across which the participants could not communicate and interact with one another except through virtual collaboration.

Vendors offer a variety of ICT tools with various technical functions, making it difficult to choose an appropriate ICT tool for a knowledge network, since not all technical functions are needed by the knowledge network members (Raimann, 2002). Each knowledge network is unique and the members' communication and interaction needs depend on the unique technical functions required by the specific network, although the appropriate ICT tool with the corresponding required functions will not exists as such (Wenger, 2001). You therefore have to decide which functions are indispensable, nice to have, or unnecessary.

In order to substitute face-to-face communication and interaction, the ICT tools functions required by the knowledge network members can be divided into several services, such as communication and coordination supporting services or content services. One service can contain a larger number of functions. The totality of services results in a service model (Raimann, 2002) that provides a framework for a knowledge network supported by ICT tools. A service model therefore provides the means with which to evaluate and prioritize ICT tools.

One of the major services needed by a knowledge network is the communication and coordination support service. Communication is the key component for sharing business- and experience-related information among the knowledge network participants. Whereas the first phases of the knowledge network life cycle largely depend on face-to-face communication, electronic communication tools gain more importance in the course of the knowledge network life cycle. A coordination service further enhances the work in a knowledge network. This service covers the workflow functions that support the accomplishment of activities, as well as personal and group calendars.

The work in a knowledge network is not only based on communication and coordination. Knowledge network members also need to have access to existing information in databases, documents, and skills. Furthermore, they have to place their externalized knowledge at the disposal of the entire company. Content services meet these needs through content structuring by means of topic grouping, content redaction, the release of documents and the syndication of documents through the multiple utilization of information (Christ, 2001).

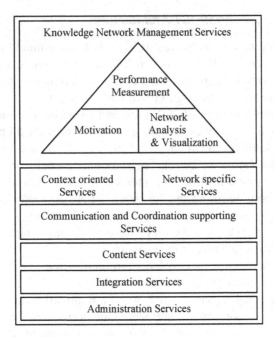

Fig. 5.3 Service Model (Source: Raimann, 2002, p. 179)

Knowledge network management services provide a way of discerning work, relations, and the outcomes of a knowledge network faster. For instance, complex performance measurement systems, like the balanced scorecard, can be built on the basis of ICT tools (Norton, 2000). On the other hand, a rudimentary way of measurement provides user tracking, which evaluates and visualizes a user's interaction behavior.

Since knowledge network members should share a common context, like a shared language, or professional background, the context services are also needed to support the interaction between and the cooperation of members in their mutual context. These services are provided by the personalization of the graphic user interface, yellow pages and directory services, an awareness of the members' activities, and feedback mechanisms.

Knowledge networks and their participants are not detached from the organizational context, the participants might also be a part of another knowledge network, while the knowledge network is only a part of a company-wide knowledge management initiative. The integration of the knowledge network activities not only covers the technical integration, but also an organizational and cultural context. These aspects of integration are embodied in the integration service and feature in integration mechanisms, e.g., portals, web-rings, and knowledge maps.

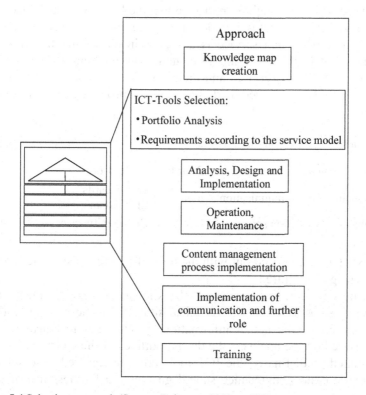

Fig. 5.4 Selection approach (Source: Raimann, 2002, p. 219)

Since most of the services concentrate on locating and transferring knowledge, typical network services might enable the generation of knowledge through, for instance, e-learning tools (Raimann, 2002).

In most cases, the above-mentioned services need to be administered. Someone or something has to determine the access rights to the chat room or guide the interaction and communication in virtual spaces. These kinds of functions are covered by the administration services.

The cornerstone service is the intranet service, which is compromised of the security, scalability, flexibility, transparency, and reliability of the ICT tools.

The selection approach (see Fig. 5.4) begins with a knowledge map creation, which ought to reveal the personal and codified knowledge within the knowledge network. The ICT tool selection depends on the company's strategy, the existing infrastructure, costs etc. A systematic approach enables the appropriate selection, therefore a portfolio analysis can help to allocate the resources. For instance, if the knowledge network has a high strategic significance, then a high resource allocation is justifiable.

The subsequent steps ought to narrow down the list of ICT tools needed and the service model helps by identifying the functions needed for a knowledge network. Each service is analyzed in terms of whether it is needed and what ICT tools it should contain. The outcome of the procedure is a priority list of services and their derived functions to be used in the knowledge network. Based on these insights, a product selection can be carried out.

Table 5.1 Example of communication services

Requirement	Priority	Realization
Synchronous communication	high	Whiteboards Chat Room
Shared information spaces	low	Community spaces

The next steps are carried out with the help of IT specialists, since technical knowledge is required.

After having determined the needs of the knowledge network members, the following steps ascertain the technical situation in the company. The analysis determines the actual information systems and technical infrastructure. Based on the analysis, the design outlines of the technical issues are ascertained, and, finally, the ICT tools are implemented. The subsequent operation and maintenance should guarantee a faultless use of the ICT tools.

The following three steps analyze and realize the technical side of cooperation and interaction of the knowledge network members.

- The first step ought to reveal how to deal with the codified and externalized knowledge. Thus, the content management process has to facilitate the actualization, creation and examination of the content created by the knowledge network members.
- The second step defines the virtual interaction between the knowledge network members. Apart from the face-to-face meetings, virtual cooperation too needs to play a role. This role might be identical to the role of the face-to-face meetings. Besides these roles, technical roles have to be established, e.g., the role of an administrator.
- The last step of the ICT tool implementation is an adequate training and an introduction to the ICT tools. Although they are crucial for success, people are sometimes reluctant to use new technologies and should be trained to do so.

Innovation

- In an innovation network, the participants perform four tasks related to the innovation, i.e. the coordination of the participants, exchange and support of information, the promotion of creativity and the development of a network. ICT tools can only be helpful in increasing the efficiency in the innovation process if their application is appropriate to its task.
- The coordination of the participants and the exchange of information require information richness, which is based on explicit knowledge. It is important that all information is available in all locations where the network participants may find themselves. Daily communication can take place via e-mail and the exchange of technical information can occur via databases, CAD systems and remote file-sharing systems.
- The promotion of creativity and the development of a network require the participants' physical presence and both are based on implicit knowledge. Communication between and direct interaction of the participants are also required. The participants' virtual communication should be ensured by ICT tools such as video conferencing and groupware.

Customer Integration

- The ICT tools are often the only link between customers and the firm, as the latter two are geographically separated from each other, and the customers' time resources for the network are very restricted. Existing ICT tools cover a wide a range of supportive tools, including:
  - Communication and co-ordination such as messaging/e-mail, workflow management, conference systems and learning platforms.
  - Management tools.
  - Intelligent tools such as categorization and problem solving.
  - Integration and database tools: databases, data warehousing and repositories.
- In the case of a customer network, it seems that the ICT tools provided for the network and available to the customers for use in their routine work, motivate them to join the network. Our research has indicated that an intranet-secured collaboration zone is mostly the first tool to be selected in compliance with the first short-term tasks and budget of the network. The capabilities of the system usually serve to ensure both information exchange and communication between members.

Mergers & Acquisition Integration

- ICT tools are enablers of the work in the knowledge network. The main interaction and cooperation should occur during face-to-face meetings. Nevertheless, ICT tools that create an electronic space, independent of time and space, for the group's purposes, also constitute a helpful means and facilitate their work.
- An M&A entails a reorganization of the involved companies and this means that employees have to work with people whom they have never worked with before, although they perform similar duties and might have similar challenges and fields of interest. Expert directories provide the means of finding people with the required knowledge.
- Take into account that before the merger or acquisitions the companies may have used different systems, which could impede the implementation of ICT tools on the technical, cultural and organizational level.

Facilitate Relationships with the Outside World

The aim of this section is to extend the network's link with its outside world. The main issue is, however, to link the network's activities with the company's business processes to prevent the network from becoming a knowledge island. The outcome of this step should be a sound relationship between the network and the outside world, which does not isolate the network, but integrates it into the knowledge flow of the organization.

Provide or Broker Support for Internal Network Initiatives and Integrate with Other Functions

Why this is important:

- Many organizational structures can support knowledge management, e.g. communities of practices, communities of interest, task forces and networks. Those structures are set up by different departments or people, not only by the knowledge management department, in order to share knowledge, and these structures exist across the company. To gain the most value and to prevent the reinvention of the wheel, it is necessary to connect the network with the rest of the company through people, ICT tools and joint events.

Innovation

- The original membership of the network is dominated by R&D experts. However, an innovation process is not isolated from the other value chains and departments. The connection to marketing provides knowledge on customers' demands. The connection to the engineering and manufacturing departments enables, e.g., verification whether the new product can be produced with the existing equipment.
- In multi-national companies one can observe a trend towards a decentralized R&D process (Gassmann and von Zedtwitz, 1998). To prevent the reinvention of the wheel and to save financial resources, the innovation networks ought to be connected to other, similar, structures. Regular face-to-face or virtual meetings with innovation network leaders, and well-known experts and gatekeepers, also enable the exchange of experiences and ideas. Additionally, redundancies in competencies are a potential source of retaining key knowledge. One the other hand, a connection to a central technology and innovation department can control the various innovation projects through the harmonization of innovation modules, the definition of work packages and the coordination of innovation activities.
- Despite the opportunity to save resources and gain efficiency in the innovation process, the independence of R&D sites could impede cooperation. You should therefore take the power structure of the company into account.
- The involvement of other business divisions depends on the life cycle of the innovation network. The involvement required by business divisions related to the outcomes of the network, usually takes place at a later stage of the network's existence, and the initiator business division may also be changed over time. The network will increasingly pay attention to the external environment and may intensify its external cooperation later on, since the participants should establish trusting relationships and coordinate their own field of action.

Customer Integration

- The customer network will provide the company with very valuable knowledge that has been derived from the customers. To integrate this knowledge within the company, the network interaction is only the first step. It is crucial to integrate other departments that can learn from the customers' experience as well as to integrate their knowledge in their initiatives. Not everybody in the company who needs the customers' knowledge can be part of the network. We therefore suggest that the network's discussions and results should be frequently communicated in the form of newsletter to interested or crucial parts of the company, such as the customer support or marketing divisions.

- Communication should come from the network as an organization and should involve all members by first discussing what to communicate to the outside world and what not. In the case of a customer network, the outside world also involves the customers' company, therefore the type of communication and the style must be appropriate for this purpose, i.e.
    - Very professional.
    - Focused on results and useful information.
    - Pointing out the status and future work etc.
- Networking between networks is also crucial for spreading knowledge to the right people. It might be interesting for the network members to hear about the work that other networks or communities do, but it is counterproductive to focus more on "outside" work than sharing your own knowledge. Do not forget that the customers involved in the networks are the most important and valuable source of knowledge for your company.
- Since the customers within the network are the crucial source of knowledge, you should be careful of integrating too many external people too often. Although it is useful to get some expert input if you need it, the network should be clearly focused on exchanging valuable customer knowledge and an integration of other external knowledge will mean time lost that could have been spent on this primary task.
- As mentioned before, in terms of the highest value for the company, it is crucial for the success of the network to integrate the acquired customer knowledge in all appropriate fields where it is needed within your company. A professional communication plan should therefore be drawn up from the very beginning. ICT tools too might help with the designing of intranet pages that should include all important network results and current topics. Frequent presentations by the network leader to management boards and departments also represent good knowledge sharing with other functions.

Mergers & Acquisition Integration

- One of the key people during the M&A process is an integration manager, since he is responsible for the overall technical and organizational integration during the post-merger phase. His insights can lead to the appropriate field of action for the M&A integration network. It is therefore important to communicate your network activities to the integration manager and align the network's work with his integration approaches.

- The work within this kind of M&A integration network is part of a bigger integration endeavor throughout the whole company. The isolation of the work within the network would contradict its purpose of integrating the people from the different companies. You should, therefore, create a connection to other integration approaches and projects.
- Besides the integration manager, communication with the functional line managers ensures the proliferation of the work done. The regular promotion of the successes of the knowledge network work increases acceptance of the M&A within the company.
- If this network initiative is the first network within the company, there might be mistrust of such an initiative. It is therefore important that the work done in the network is successful and that the success is communicated to the company to provide an example.

 Steps to get you there:

1. The knowledge network initiator, i.e. a person, group of people or a business unit, should develop sufficient internal capabilities to help business units accurately interpret their needs and find the right type of help to respond to these needs.
2. The initiator should be positioned to identify key issues across business units, help evaluate and select appropriate education and consulting resources, and assess which methods and external partners are most effective and why.
3. Typical ways in which the initiator can support business units, include:
   - Contact the business unit senior management and knowledge management leaders to help them interpret how knowledge management challenges relate to the business unit strategy and performance objectives.
   - Develop a network of consulting and education experts on a variety of topics related to knowledge management and knowledge networks as part of the network's ongoing participation in an external knowledge management community.
   - Broker contacts and help negotiate contracts with a range of consulting and education resources based on the specific needs and preferences of business unit clients.

Establish Internal Measurement

In this last step in setting up knowledge networks for growth we need to think about the term 'measure' since you can only measure what you can manage. This step describes the potential opportunities to internally measure the network, which will be explained in more detail in the article following these guidelines. Despite the difficulty associated with the measurement of knowledge, some factors can indicate whether the performance of the knowledge network is declining or not. The performance, in turn, depends on various factors such as the members' motivation and the execution of the work.

Choose and Organize Appropriate Rewards or Incentives

Reward and incentive systems can motivate the participants to contribute better to the network. Appropriate reward and incentive systems depend on the company culture and are therefore very company specific. However, there are some issues that apply to all companies when motivating network members to contribute to the network.

Why this is important:

- Rewards and incentives contribute to people's motivation and motivation is the key driver for all human activities. It has two dimensions.
  - Motivation can be extrinsic, and therefore it could be proactively governed from outside by an appropriate reward or incentive systems.
  - Motivation can be intrinsic, meaning that people are motivated by appreciation of their work and not by material means.
- A knowledge network depends on its participants and their motivation for contributing to the network and for cooperating with one another. The question of motivation for cooperation is

especially important in a knowledge network for growth, since this requires people from different companies to cooperate.

Innovation

- The reward and incentive systems in an innovation network are strongly related to the network's field of action, since the solution of the task to be solved can improve the efficiency of the daily business.
- Financial rewards and incentives can backfire and destroy the transfer of implicit knowledge, because the quantification of implicit knowledge is difficult and an appropriate quid pro quo can not be established.

Customer Integration

- Since, the members of the customer network come from different companies that have to pay for the company's products and services, the question of reward and incentive systems for a customer network is a pivotal issue for the transfer of knowledge.
- Financial reward systems are not always the appropriate means, since very often a company is not willing to pay its customers. The participation in a network ought to be motivated by their managers' recognition and the value created for their daily work.
- Task-related solutions, like understanding the problem solutions earlier than other customers and establishing stronger ties with the company, also provide the required motivation.

Mergers & Acquisition Integration

- Very often employees have experienced various reorganizations during the post-merger integration. Furthermore, employees are reluctant to share their knowledge, since they are scared of becoming superfluous. After the M&A they might even regard the other company's employees as the enemy. Much motivation of the network participants is therefore required.
- During the meetings an appropriate atmosphere is significant in order to overcome the participants' anxieties. Since involvement in a knowledge network should be based on intrinsic motivation, this could lead to being regarded as an expert, which would, in turn, result in a higher self-esteem. The clear communication of the objectives of the network facilitates commitment to it.

Steps to get you there:

1. Primarily a knowledge network serves to share implicit knowledge. *Intrinsic* motivation is more important than *extrinsic* motivation when you want to transfer implicit knowledge (Frey and Osterloh, 2000). It is therefore important to ask potential members whether they wish to participate and cooperate within a knowledge network even before the network has been set up.
2. It should be taken into account that monetary rewards for individuals can backfire, since the network members not rewarded can feel that they have been discriminated against. Rewards can create a sense of unfairness, especially if the knowledge network leader has not defined clear rules for the reward process (Wenger et al., 2002). It has also been observed that rewarding, i.e. extrinsic motivation, could impede knowledge sharing and collaboration (Stajkovic and Luthans, 2001).
3. The reward and incentive system depends on the company or even the business unit's culture and structure. Therefore, consider and compare the systems before the setup of the knowledge network.
4. If you have to deliver material rewards and incentives, set clear criteria to achieve a reward and/or incentive and communicate these to all involved.
5. Motivation can be achieved by appreciation of work done in a knowledge network. The communication of success and participants' contribution can especially enhance self-esteem.
6. Appreciation of the contribution of the network by the local home organization of the network can be a strong motivator.

In order to comprehend members' preferences, it is the best to ask themselves. Therefore, conduct interviews – a template of interview guidelines provides the first steps[23].

Methodology at a Glance: The Project Plan

The project plan is aimed at providing a detailed description of the steps required for building a network.

---

[23] See subchapter Interview Guidelines

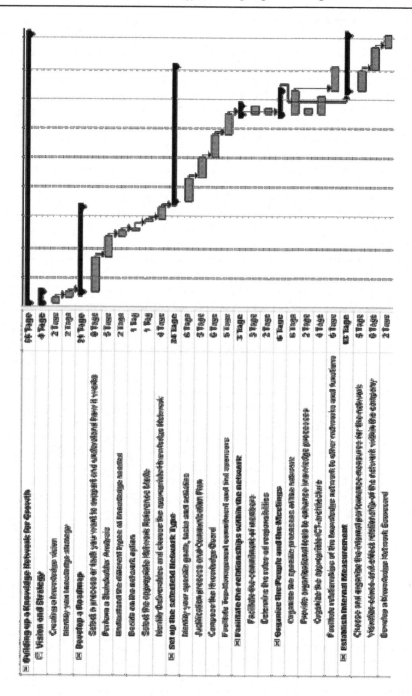

Fig. 5.5 Project plan for building up knowledge networks for growth

6 Integrated Performance Measurement System for Knowledge Networks for Growth

Ellen Enkel, Maria Rumyantseva and Grzegorz Gurgul

Research Center KnowledgeSource, University of St. Gallen, Switzerland

Introduction

In economically hard times the call to prove value in respect of costs is getting louder. Management would like to see a relationship between cost and value and return on investment (ROI). It is crucial to prove performance and value in order to get the attention and support that activities, especially knowledge management activities, need. Beside this, performance measurement has always been significant for the monitoring of action – a precondition for optimization – and demonstrating areas of improvement in order to adjust this action to make it even more successful.

From a knowledge perspective, performance measurement has always been needed, but never sufficiently achieved. On the one hand, the nature of knowledge makes it difficult to identify with performance indicators. How can one prove how much new knowledge has been created before it is represented in new products and services? On the other hand, knowledge management has always served as a supporting process for business processes, has never existed for its own sake. Improvement of business processes regarding efficiency, innovation or risk management can thus be seen as a result of successful knowledge management action (von Krogh et al., 2001b). But, besides knowledge, other supporting activities claim to be responsible for better results and the achievement of business goals. Yet there is nearly no way of isolating the supporting influence of knowledge activities on a company's success or, even more difficult, on growth achievements.

Besides the characteristics of knowledge and the supporting nature of knowledge management, knowledge management activities are always a complex set of initiatives trying to influence the complex system called 'a company' positively. Knowledge management activities achieve middle- and long-term goals rather than short-term business goals, which reduces the number of metrics that can be meaningfully used.

It could be that the approach of searching for the one, unique performance measurement instrument is a blind alley. Research as well as practice needs to search for more individual approaches that also meet individual company needs and specific knowledge activities. Based on this understanding of a more individual approach, this article will try to develop a focused knowledge network performance measurement system, combining different single metrics within one integrated measurement system. The idea is that the appropriate combination of metrics, which are deficient when used separately, and a strong focus on one knowledge management activity – the knowledge network for growth – will lead to a comprehensive performance measurement system.

The aim of the integrated measurement system is to first illustrate the value of the network set-up in achieving company growth, and, secondly, to include instruments to monitor this action as well as helping to adjust and optimize it. This integrated measurement system can be divided into two parts: the internal and the external performance measurement. The internal performance measurement includes instruments for the monitoring of the network from an internal (network) perspective. The external performance measurement shows the knowledge scorecard, which has been derived from a balanced scorecard approach (BSC), as an instrument with which to reveal value on a external (corporate) level (see Vassiliadis et al., 2000).

Consequently, the following section will first discuss different performance measurement approaches divided into direct and indirect metrics in keeping with their focus on and value for knowledge networks. A presentation and discussion of the new integrated performance measurement system for knowledge networks for growth will follow.

Discussing Selected Performance Measurement Approaches

In recent years many firms as well as academics have tried to develop measurement methods in which knowledge is measured against other resources, or in which the focus is wholly on measuring knowledge. These activities resulted in an increased number of methods for measuring knowledge, but they are all based on different concepts and there is no single, universally accepted method. In the following section, several methods will be presented to provide an overview of the available methods.

There are indirect and direct methods for measuring knowledge and knowledge activities. Indirect measurement means to define measures or indicators for knowledge and knowledge activities from secondary indicators (e.g., financial indicators), whereas direct measures try to measure 'knowledge' itself, or the relation between the participation in a network and the performance of a related business unit or project team. With this distinction in mind, a few selected methods are briefly presented.

Indirect Measurement Methods

Tobin's Q

Concept: *Value of intangible assets = Market value – replacement value of tangible assets*

Tobin's Q is based on the observation that knowledge-intensive companies have a higher market value than a value in terms of tangible assets and that the market recognizes the value of intangible assets (see Quinn, 1992). Tobin's Q therefore calculates the difference between the book value of a company and the replacement cost of the company's assets and calls this the intangible assets value.

Management Value Added

Concept: *Knowledge capital = Management Value Added (what is left after all costs have been accounted for) / Price of Capital*

This measurement as defined by Strassmann, stresses the importance of management activity (see Strassmann, 1996). Strassmann defines knowledge capital as the result of management value added (that which is left after all costs have been accounted for) in relation to the price of capital.

Direct Measurement Methods

Social Network Analysis

Social Network Analysis (SNA) is a widely used method in social science and proliferates in other disciplines like economics, marketing, and industrial engineering (Parker et al., 2001). The core idea behind the measurement method is that the outcomes of networks are not a static state, but rather the effect of the relationship between the network participants and interdependencies between people and relations. Social network analysis can be used to visualize network performance or help to monitor it – even in a rather limited manner focusing on internal relations between the network members.

A quantitative[24] and a qualitative approach can be used to perform an SNA (Cross et al., 2002). In the following, a quantitative approach is outlined in which the first step consists of visualizing and understanding the relationships between network members. The visualization of the relationships is based on written inquiries and interviews in which the knowledge network leader concentrates on the degree of communication and interaction between the knowledge network members.

The outcome is a network diagram that illustrates the relationships between the knowledge network members and describes the status of the relationships. The diagram shows the key people, valuable knowledge owners, peripheral persons who do not want to or can not interact or participate, and network subgroups that could be indicative of a split in the knowledge network.

Based on the actual situation within the network or on the relationships between the members, measures can be executed to improve the desired relationships through, e.g., social events in which the crucial people are brought together.

Return on Investment

The Return on Investment (ROI) provides a quantitative view of the knowledge network outcomes. The ROI has two parts, namely the costs and the benefits, and both have to be captured in order to perform the measurement. The costs of each stage of the development of the knowledge network initiatives can be easily allotted, since they include personal costs such as time spent in meetings, infrastructure costs such as maintaining of the ICT tools, or the expenditure on face-to-face meetings.

The benefits, however, are less obvious, since the outcomes of the knowledge network are created within cross-company or cross-business unit groups that proliferate in various companies (a customer knowledge network) or business units (an M&A knowledge network). Thus the benefits of a knowledge network can only be estimated (Wenger, 2002). For in-

---

[24] The qualitative approach is beyond the scope of the outline. The reader interested in an in-depth understanding of the qualitative approach is referred to Wasserman and Faust (Wasserman and Faust, 1994) for an introduction.

stance, a company improves a product, which creates a certain value for the whole company. The knowledge network members in a customer knowledge network are also, to a certain degree, involved in the improvement of the product. The benefit of a knowledge network is therefore a part of the total value for the company and can be estimated as:

Benefit of the knowledge network = Value for the whole company * the proportion of the knowledge network * the degree of certainty that the value was created within the knowledge network. The degree of certainty and the relevant proportion of the knowledge network can only be determined by interviewing the knowledge network members.

Anecdotal Evidence

The anecdotal evidence is based on two pillars: revealing the cause-effect connection and the systematic collection of the cause-effect connections (Wenger, 2002).

The first pillar consists of storytelling with knowledge network members about their activities in which three significant questions act as criteria of the activities: What was the challenge to be solved? What was the solution contributed by the knowledge network? How was the solution realized in order to generate value?

The second pillar is the systematic collection of the cause-effect connections of all activities of the knowledge network. Only a systematic collection guarantees the reliability of the measurement, therefore the knowledge network leader should execute periodic and frequent surveys, or carry out interviews in order to gather the information needed.

Human Resource Accounting

Concept: *Expected Realizable Value = Definition of service states (job) +*
Determination of value of each state to the organization +
Estimation of tenure in organization +
Probability of occupying status +
Discounting future cash-flow

This method encompasses several different measurement approaches. One approach is the Stochastic Rewards Valuation Model that measures the expected conditional and realizable value of an individual to an organization (see Flamholtz, 1989).

Balanced Scorecard (BSC)

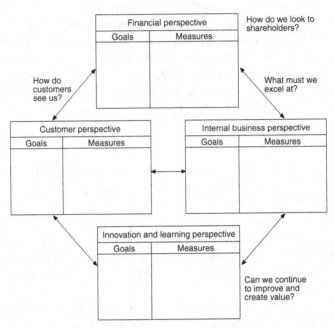

Fig. 6.1 The Balanced Scorecard (Kaplan and Norton 1992, p. 72)

Probably the best-known direct performance measurement method combining both quantitative and qualitative indicators is a balance scorecard (BSC) (Kaplan and Norton, 1992). The BSC is basically a measurement system comprised of four perspectives that are critical for a company. The first perspective is the company's *internal processes* that are directly responsible for the company's performance.

The tangible results of the internal processes are reflected in the second perspective – the company's *financial outcomes*. Apparently, financial indicators alone can not provide complete information on the firm's development, and, more importantly, on its potential for future progress. The latter is mirrored by the forth perspective that comprises *learning and growth* indicators. A combination of the three described perspectives is not entirely valid without the independent external indicators, such as *customer* feedback and actions (fourth perspective), which increase the method's validity.

The combination of financial and non-financial indicators, reflecting both the outcomes and processes, growth potential as well as interactions with the external environment, shifts the method from an improved measurement system to a comprehensive strategic management system.

The interlinkages between the measurements offered by each of four perspectives give the method a critical advantage above other measurement systems. The chain of causes and effects allows all four perspectives to be analyzed together (see Fig. 6.2).

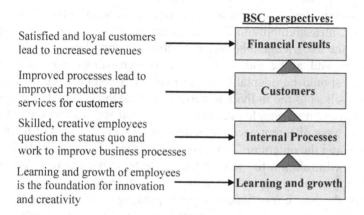

Fig. 6.2 The Balanced Scorecard and knowledge management (Arveson, 1999)

In a balanced scorecard, the company is approached from the development perspective. The cause-and-effect chain is built from learning, which stimulates improvements in the processes, such as improving products and services and increasing customer satisfaction. In turn, these improvements through increased demand increase the firm's revenues and therefore its financial outcomes.

The cause-and-effect chain also implies that non-financial indicators are reflected in financial indicators, as they are all interdependent.

The dynamics of the company development implies that all four perspectives will change in time, therefore creating a kind of development loop. The company's learning and growth could be the basis for the next loop in the company's development.

Discussion of Approaches

Measuring intangible assets like knowledge is difficult because of the nature of knowledge and knowledge management as a supportive process as well as because of the middle- to long-term goals that knowledge management try to attain. The single metrics described above try to illustrate the value of knowledge management, or single knowledge-related activities on company performance, but can't be used to visualize network performance, or help the network leader to monitor it.

When discussing measurement tools, three criteria need to be taken into account: First, measurement tools should illustrate the cause-and-effect relationship of the knowledge management activity within the chain of business processes, and, at the end, in the company's growth strategy. Second, the measures should be adaptable to the individual company culture and structure as well as to the individual network approach chosen. Third, performance measurement should take into account that stakeholders, like top management, have different needs than network leaders in terms of the degree of detail and the outcome. Top management needs to see the influence of the network in relation to the company's strategy, but network leaders need to identify areas of improvement on a network level.

Neither of the above-mentioned single approaches fulfill these criteria, therefore, a new, integrated, measurement system for knowledge networks for growth will be presented in the next section.

The Integrated Performance Measurement System for Knowledge Networks for Growth

Introduction

The integrated performance measurement system for knowledge networks for growth has been constructed using external and internal performance measurements. Only a combination of measures showing the performance from an external (corporate) and an internal (network) perspective can provide a holistic view of the network performance and value creation.

The *external performance measurements* contain a knowledge scorecard since an external measurement instrument can be used to implement and monitor a growth strategy that knowledge networks should support. The knowledge scorecard, based on the balanced scorecard approach that was presented in the previous section, needs to be adapted to comply with the network's specific focus on knowledge and the aims it tries fulfill. The knowledge scorecard therefore needs to be made up of meaningful indicators directly derived from the network action or related to them. Complexity management can help to identify these indicators.

But a scorecard will not help to monitor the internal network performance, or help the network leader to identify weaknesses and areas of improvement. Therefore it needs to be combined with *internal performance measures* that are comprised of several single metrics. One of these, is the newly developed individual network performance survey (INPS). The INPS can be used to identify weaknesses with regards to the tasks that the network should solve within the structure of the network. The idea is that the network members can best judge if the components of their network are supportive or need to be improved.

On a more detailed level another of the performance measures is the health check that aims to help the network leader to check if the network is healthy or not. In order to provide an answer, questions are formulated that relate to the major components of the network. The answers to these questions point out weaknesses and areas of improvement. The health check helps the network leader to monitor the network internal's health, while the IPMS measures the effectiveness of the network's tasks. Combining both the individual network performance survey and the health check will help to identify weaknesses and areas of improvement.

External Performance Measurement

Systems Thinking to Visualize the Cause-and-Effect of Networks

The most difficult task in creating a balanced scorecard is to identify meaningful indicators that are really derived from network activity and therefore show the influence of network activities on the fulfilling of business goals. The challenges that were presented in the introduction, such as the complexity of knowledge management activity, the difficulty of identifying the value provided by a supporting activity when there are also other variables, and the characteristics of knowledge, make it difficult to identify indicators that prove network action.

Systems thinking as part of complexity management is aimed at understanding the cause-and-effect relationship of complex systems (Senge, 1990; Probst and Gomez, 1991). Knowledge management activities, and especially knowledge network activities, are complex systems because they consist of many activities that depend on different variables, some of which can not be influenced directly. An example should clarify this challenge.

A knowledge network aiming to support innovation needs to consist of appropriate members. These members need to be motivated to share their knowledge, create new knowledge and engage themselves in supportive innovation activities to create value. The members' motivation is influenced by many factors, like the personal value that they receive from their network participation, their relationships with the other members, the recognition or support that the management gives them, and the working environment of the network. These influencing factors can also be private factors such as their fear of losing their jobs. Some of these factors can be influenced directly, some only indirectly, while other can't be influenced at all. Remembering that the component "member" is only one of many components in the network structure, makes it easier to imagine a knowledge network as a complex system integrated into an even more complex system, the company. Therefore to understand and influence this system, complexity management methods seem the most appropriate when dealing with knowledge networks.

Illustrating the cause-and-effect relationship of a knowledge network has three benefits in terms of performance measurement.

- It can be used to visualize benefits and influence various factors of the network's activity within the company. Although networks can only influence a limited part of the cause-and-effect-cycle directly, members should think about the other steps as well by means of communication and influencing (e.g., by integration in their communication plan).
- It will help to identify meaningful indicators needed for the development of a knowledge scorecard.
- It will help to identify activities that can leverage the achievement of the proposed goals of the network.

The approach followed to visualize the cause-and-effect relationship of network action is adapted from Honegger's writings on networks (2001) and based on the work of Gomez and Probst (1991). Honegger (2002) recommends a six-step approach in dealing with complex systems:

1. Identification of the perspectives.
2. Distinguishing of key factors.
3. Creating a first cause-and-effect cycle.
4. Development of a cause-and-effect network.
5. Interpretation of the relationships.
6. Derivation of activities.

This approach should be followed in a team context that involves the important stakeholders. Only a team can take several perspectives as well as the knowledge needed to create a cause-and-effect network into account. Understanding the different perspectives will also lead to better cooperation in future.

The first step *Identification of the perspectives* serves to clarify the different perspectives regarding the complex system, in our case an innovation knowledge network. Questions such as the following will help with the identification process: Who are the stakeholders and what are they aiming at? Which are the departments involved and what is their aim? What is the perspective of the network member or the network leader? Who is the "owner" or sponsor of the network and what is he aiming at?

Identifying these different perspectives and different goals will help to identify important variables, which will build the basis of the later cause-and-effect network. The next step is to reduce the perspectives and, by doing so, decide which of them are important and need to be taken into account in further work.

Thereafter it is important to distinguish the key factors that are important from the different perspectives. These key factors, or network variables, are derived from the goals and aims of the different stakeholders identified in the previous step. In the case of an innovation knowledge network, e.g., the goal and aims might be: the sponsors wants to support the innovation rate in his business unit in relation to his budget for the following year, the marketing and sales manager wants to improve the quality of the products and services and increase their sales rate, and the network members want to work in exciting new fields, earn recognition and get to know new people inside the organization. Every stakeholder therefore has his own goals or hopes pertaining to the network, which need to be taken into account.

A first central cause-and-effect cycle can be created with the essential factors identified by the previous step. In adapting this method to an innovation network, the cause-and-effect cycle can be illustrated as shown by the following figure (see Fig. 6.3).

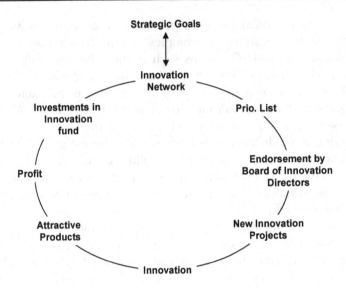

Fig. 6.3 First cause-and-effect cycle of an innovation network

Starting with the innovation network: its main task is to discuss new corporate innovation projects in terms of their potential for the company as well as in terms of how they fit in with the company's strategic goals (e.g., growth through innovation in a specific area). The innovation network members provide the board of directors with a list of projects that they recommend for support. In their frequent meetings, the board of directors discuss the proposed projects and decide (following the recommendations of the innovation network) which projects will be supported (financially and in terms of resources) and which not. If the decision is positive, the innovation network obtains its funding and this will lead to new innovation for more attractive products or services. In a best case scenario, the latter leads to higher profits that can be reinvested in the innovation fund which finances the company's innovation projects. Consequently, more innovation projects can then be funded in the following years, providing the company with an opportunity to generate value innovation (see Drucker, 2002) and growth by, e.g., conquering new market segments with new products and services.

This rather simple first cycle illustrates the cause-and-effect at which the network initiator is aiming, or the value that the innovation network needs to create. But the innovation network does not exist in a vacuum and it is naturally influenced by its corporate surroundings, e.g. the company culture and structure in which it is integrated. Consequently, the next step is to identify the surroundings of the network, e.g., where the innovation project ideas that need to be discussed come from, or what influence other network actions have on it. These factors need to be integrated to create a holistic picture of the existing cause-and-effect relationships.

In our example, the innovation network, the ideas for discussion could come from, e.g., its members who are portfolio managers for a product group situated in different regions, or from other company employees as a result of, e.g., corporate entrepreneurship, or from external sources like customers or external research centers. Other ideas and feedback on innovation come from the marketing and sales divisions as well as from the support and service department. They have connections with customers, competitors and the market and can provide feedback on areas of improvement in services and products as well as on customer requirements that have not yet been fully fulfilled. Gradually, the cause-and-affect network becomes more detailed, as Fig. 6.4 shows.

The degree of detail should be in proportion to the importance of the factors – do they really influence the innovation network cycle? – and the transparency that the cause-and-effect network should retain – too many factors will make it hard to understand the relationships, transparency will be lost. It is also necessary to ensure that only existing relationships are created and not future constructs or effects that don't as yet exist in real life.

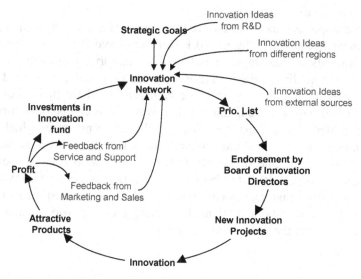

Fig. 6.4 The cause-and-effect network becomes more substantial

The next step is the *interpretation of the relationships* as they materialize in the network. According to Honneger (2002, p. 26 ff.) this should be done by indicating how direct (time-wise) and strong (how directly related) the effect of a cause is. One important part of the interpretation process is to *identify the lever* that can influence the attaining of the proposed results. In our example, the ideas from the different parts of the organization will only be transferred to the network members if there is a link to these parts of the organization as well as to other sources of knowledge.

As can be seen in Figure 6.5, the linkage builds the necessary precondition for the transfer of ideas for innovation projects to the network members. Only if this linkage exists, will the network members have all knowledge needed to make decisions, to reduce the risk of undertaking wrong innovation initiatives, to improve efficiency by reducing redundancies in innovation, and to focus on the innovation needed to achieve the company's growth strategy.

One other major identified lever is the quality of the meetings as well as the work of the network. Only if the innovation networks create results of a high quality, in our example the list of innovation projects that require support, will the innovation rate within the company increase and the proposed profit be reached. The quality of the network activities can be influenced by many initiatives.

One important factor to ensure the quality of a network is the *appropriate members*. Only if the network members have the knowledge to judge the innovation ideas by their potential to support the company objectives and by the quality of the idea proposed, can they make the right decisions. The network members need to be *motivated* to share their knowledge – which will improve the quality of their work. This can be done through the management support that they receive, the environment in which the network ought to work and the personal values that the network action creates for its members. One supportive factor of motivation is the empowerment of the network: only if the board of innovation directors follows the recommendations that the network makes, and, therefore, respect its work, are the network members motivated to share their knowledge and will the network attract the appropriate members.

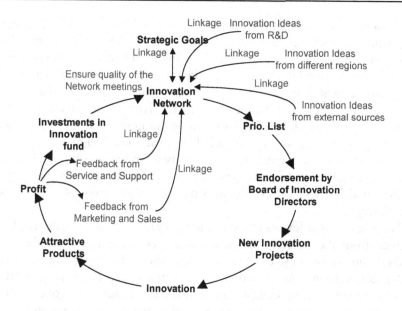

Fig. 6.5 Identification of levers to influence the cause-and-effect relationships

One last point to clarify the above-mentioned prerequisites is the knowledge base to which the networks need to connect. The network members need to know about the existing innovation projects – whether they are in an active mode or have been completed – to base their decisions on information available, to reduce redundancy and be able to create synergies. This requires a database or instrument with which to keep track of innovation projects and their status within the company. Only transparency can ensure that the goals described above will be reached and can also facilitate learnings from projects undertaken.

The identified levers *linkage* and *quality of the network meetings* can be influenced directly and indirectly. Thus, the next step in following the complexity approach is to derive activities from the interpretation of network relationships. As seen above, single actions can influence these levers quite effectively and ensure that the proposed goals are reached. Besides a concrete activity plan to improve the network effects, indicators need to be found to measure the change in performance. The indicators can be found by using the activities and levers identified.

In our example of the innovation network, indicators such as the number of ideas transferred to the network members, or the number of innovation project proposals that they discuss at every meeting can be seen as an indicator of whether the linkage exists and can be improved through the proposed activities. The quality of the meetings can be indicated by the members who take part, e.g., in a self-assessment or by the number of members who come to the meetings (personally, they do not send a representative). Also feedback from the marketing and sales department can serve as a long-term indicator, e.g., if the new product, created through the innovation project, garners significant profit or receives positive feedback from customers. A more short-term indicator is the number of innovation projects that were successfully completed. The rationale behind this is that if the network is doing a good job, the quality of the ideas supported should increase, which leads to more innovation projects successfully completed. Cost-related barriers that could impede innovation projects should then also decrease.

These are only a few examples of meaningful *indicators* that have been derived from the analysis of cause-and-effect relationships as identified through the use of complexity management methods. Proving these cause-and-effect relationships can be valuable in itself, because management as well as network members want to see how meaningful their work is and if the return on investment (the costs related to network building and maintaining) can be seen.

To prove that the network is linked to the growth strategy of the company, additional instruments need to be used. The above method provides ideal preconditions for using a knowledge scorecard to illustrate the value of the network with financial figures. The knowledge scorecard approach will be described in the following section.

Developing a Knowledge Scorecard

As described in a previous section, a traditional balanced scorecard does not measure knowledge directly. This drawback will be overcome with the intellectual capital (IC) measurement perspective of the knowledge scorecard.

The knowledge scorecard (based on Vassiliadis et al., 1999) aims to not only measure different areas of knowledge impact, such as customers and internal processes, but also different levels of impact, such as the company, the network and the individual. This is possible, because the knowledge scorecard consists of different perspectives and levels. As such it not only measures the performance of knowledge networks, it looks at the impact of a knowledge network on the achievement of the business goals, risk reduction, efficiency and innovation, which should support the corporate growth strategy.

A knowledge scorecard can be built for different levels: the enterprise, network and the individual. Consequently, measures have to be identified at each level. Five to six indicators per perspective per layer should be sufficient to articulate and measure the knowledge objectives. The following table provides an example:

Table 6.1 Example of indicators for a knowledge scorecard (Source: Back et al., 2005)

	Company	Network	Individual
Financials	• Discounted cash-flow • Sales increase • ROE, EVA, ROI	• Profits resulting from operation of KNN • % of R&D invested in basic research in KNN	• Profits resulting from individual involvement • % of input in the innovation process
Customers	• Customer satisfaction • Retention rate • Customer complaints • % of products < 3 years	• Usage of ICT • % of orders received out of total offers	• Sales per professional • Sales per salesperson • Value added per employee
Internal Processes	• Time to Market • No. of customer complaints	• % of contracts filed without error • Process cost development	• Employee turnover ratio • Degree of process task fulfilment
Growth	• Number of patents and cost of patent maintenance • Income per R&D expense • Project life-cycle cost per dollar of sales	• % of new ideas generated to new ideas implemented, • Knowledge Assets	• Number of individual entries to the data base • Qualifications, skills and motivation of employees

To develop a knowledge scorecard, success factors have to be identified from the business objective. Thereafter the identified success factors can be used to constitute performance indicators, which are closely related to the work of the network and its members. In a last step, these indicators will be assigned to the four focus areas of the knowledge scorecard. The following Figure 6.6 shows this procedure in an overview.

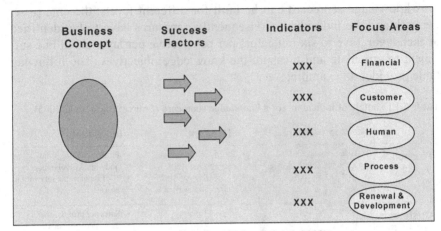

Fig. 6.6 Development of a Scorecard (Source: Raimann et al. 2000)

The knowledge scorecard aims to measure the value of knowledge activities that are related to the corporate growth strategy. All activities need to be represented by indicators with which data can be gained in order to monitor improvement on the various scorecard dimensions. The knowledge network action is only one activity of the huge number of knowledge activities that occur in a company. The scorecard thus measures the network performance indirectly by adding network-related indicators in the various perspectives.

Gaining meaningful indicators to prove network performance is crucial because it is the precondition for measuring the right elements – in our case the network activities and performance. As described before, the complexity management approach can serve to identify such meaningful indicators by analyzing the cause-and-effect relationships of the knowledge network for growth. After performing this analysis, the identified indicators need to be clustered in the knowledge scorecard according to the individual, network and company level of impact, as described before.

Following our example of the innovation network, the indicators already mentioned a need to be operationalized and clustered according to the four dimensions of the knowledge scorecard mentioned in Fig. 6.1. The *Learning and Growth* perspective of the knowledge scorecard could include indicators like the number of ideas transferred to the network members, the number of innovation project proposals that the innovation network discusses per month, or the number of innovation projects that were successfully completed.

These indicators are related to the innovation network activities, but the scorecard also needs to include other knowledge indicators with which to measure innovation improvement and company growth that are only indirectly related to network activities. Accordingly, it is difficult to illustrate network performance only through a knowledge scorecard. The scorecard needs to be combined with the cause-and-effect illustration of the previous section to show the network's influence on the proposed business goals.

Success Stories to Visualize Results

Success stories about network activities and success are becoming increasingly popular. This instrument is primarily a communication and marketing tool rather than a performance measurement method. Success stories serve to illustrate the network activities and how valuable these can be. Whereas the illustration of cause-and-effect and the knowledge scorecard aim to visualize value, they are also rather complicated techniques suitable for management, while success stories can communicate value to a broader audience through small, interesting stories.

Success stories of network activities can consequently be seen as complementing the communication of value and the gaining of management and employees' attention. Success stories are normally no longer than one page and focus on a specific activity related to a network that created a measurable impact on a company's activities.

Internal Performance Measurement

The internal measurement system consists mainly of two independent instruments that help the network leader to monitor network performance and identify the areas of improvement. The first instrument is the individual network performance survey (INPS) that measures the performance of a single network according to its outcomes. The second instrument is the health check, that can be compared with a doctor's regular health check: testing your health through questions related to important or crucial areas of your body. The health check for networks includes questions related to the major components of the network. Both instruments should be used by the network leader as they offer him an internal view of the network itself.

Individual Network Performance Survey (INPS)

Research has identified the key components that form a network (Enkel 2005). But research has also showed that in successful networks all these components (comprised in the MERLIN model) are not of an equal quality and quantity. For example, a successful knowledge network does not necessarily need a large ICT support system although some successful ones do have this. One major outcome of the research was that the quality of the components needed is related to the task that the network needs to fulfill. This outcome makes it difficult to search for one performance measurement instrument that – depending on the structure of the network – indicates whether the network performs well or needs to be improved.

Another important point that needs urgent attention is the fact that performance measures are only allocated to managers and network leaders. Network members should be regarded as persons who are willing and motivated to fulfill their tasks within the network, and we should therefore also ask them which structure, meaning the quality of the components, is most supportive and which is not.

In keeping with the above argument, a questionnaire for network members was developed which reveals the structure of the individual network with regard to the quality of the components. The questionnaire questions the network members on how supportive this structure is in terms of the network tasks. Every member of a network should complete this questionnaire, which starts with open questions on the goal and the tasks of the network, includes closed questions on the quality and the importance of the different components and closes with open questions on the success or failure of the network. The last questions on how successful the network is and why it is regarded as such, is the most significant question from which to analyze the results.

Besides this questionnaire, the individual network performance survey (INPS) contains a table with which to analyze the results of the data gained. The table is constructed of a list of core components and two columns to indicate the individual quality of each component for the specific network to which the member belongs, and the importance of these components for the task fulfillment. All the answers of one network's members are codified and summarized according to the components. Comparing the averages of the data in both columns, one obtains a clear picture of the network and areas of improvement. A difference larger than 1 indicates where the individual quality of a component doesn't meet the need of the members working in this structure (see Table 6.2). This is therefore an area of improvement.

Table 6.2 INPS Analysis

Components	Quality of the component in your network	Importance for your task fulfillment	Difference
Strong management support	Good (2)	Important (2)	0
Strong link to the corporate knowledge vision and strategy	Average (3)	Very important (1)	2
Right people in the network	Very good (1)	Very important (1)	0
Rewards and Incentives are in place for the work of the members	Average (3)	Less important (4)	1
Etc.			

The INPS allows network managers individual monitoring and adaptation of the network's task-supporting structure. The INPS doesn't monitor areas less obviously related to task fulfillment or areas of improvement that aren't a problem as yet. The latter could benefit from a more detailed health check.

Health Check

The network should undergo a regular health check. The health check contains questions with regard to single components of the network, e.g., whether all necessary roles are in place, or whether the selected tools are used properly. A negative answer indicates that in a specific area of the construction, the network did not complete the stage fully, or that important development points were forgotten or not selected carefully enough. Then, depending on the area mentioned, it is useful to check the corresponding steps in the building process again or repeat them once more.

Where Is the gap?

Network alignment with corporate vision and growth strategy/communication

- Has the strategy been clearly communicated to the top management, the relevant people such as stakeholders, the entire company and the potential/involved members?

Facilitate top management commitment/knowledge board

- Does the network get support from the top management? Do they accept it?
- Does the network get the appropriate support regarding resources such as time, attention, people and money?

Identify your goals, task and activities

- Do the network members work on a specific task or activity? Does the network fulfil a concrete goal that is derived from a specific business goal?
- Do all members know what specific task they have to fulfil in the network? Does everybody know the concrete processes that have to be executed to solve the network's operational knowledge task?
- Is the output of the knowledge processes such that the next process in line can be started?

Facilitate relationships within the network

- Are the roles and responsibilities clearly defined? Does everybody know which responsibilities are attached to each role? Is it clear who the participants in the network are? Do people know one another?
- Are the members sufficiently organized by the network leader? Are the meetings organized well?
- Do the network members show the necessary commitment? Does the network leader support this commitment?
- Are appropriate organizational tools provided in order to support the network's knowledge creation efforts?
- Is the appropriate ICT architecture in place so as to support the network's operational knowledge task? Are there communication problems associated with the ICT infrastructure?

Facilitate relationships to the outside world

- Is there a knowledge management board in place? Does it actively support the network in its activities? Does it provide it with strategic guidance? Does the board improve the effectiveness of the network?
- Does the company have a knowledge management department that

supports the network activities? Does the knowledge management department provide the network with the necessary information, for example, from other knowledge management activities in the company, to pursue its tasks?

- Are other functions of the company that have a reciprocal influence on the network's work, integrated with the network? Are there conflicts to be resolved?

Establish measurements

- Are the appropriate rewards and incentives in place to motivate an individual or a team? Are they in line with the company culture?
- Is the performance of the individual, the role and the network evaluated appropriately? Are network goals included in the personal goal system? Does the network leader look after role fulfillment and does he provide feedback?
- Is the performance of the network periodically evaluated – internally as well as externally (using the health check, symptoms of failure and the knowledge scorecard)? Is there a specific scorecard in place that translates the business goals to network goals? Do the members of the network participate in this process?
- Are they familiar with the goals? Is the fulfillment of the network goals apparent to the responsible managers?

The network leader can run through these questions periodically. If all the answers are positive, nothing needs to be done, if one or more answers are negative, the network leader knows there are areas of improvement. The questions form clusters that correspond to the main steps of the guidelines, this enables the network leader to return to this section in the guidelines and check the recommendations given. This might help him to improve the network.

The template in the following chapters can be used as a first step and instrument of the internal performance measurement[25].

---

[25] See subchapter Internal Performance Measurement System

Conclusion

This study is an attempt to address the idea of an integrated measurement system which includes a combination of external and internal metrics to illustrate and monitor network performance.

The external measurement part of the proposed integrated measurement system is based on using complexity management to visualize cause-and-effect relationships of the knowledge network for growth for the organization, which is in itself valuable to illustrate network influence on a company's growth goals. But complexity management is also used to identify levers to increase the network's value as well as to identify meaningful indicators for creating a knowledge scorecard. The knowledge scorecard, as the second instrument of the external measurement part, offers the possibility to show the network's influence on the company's growth strategy. By using meaningful indicators, derived from the analysis of the network's cause-and-effect relationships as well as from other knowledge management activities, it is possible to measure knowledge management performance in the field of interest. Visualizing the value of the network by using cause-and-effect relationships and the knowledge scorecard serves to inform management and helps the network leader to obtain sufficient support and resources. To communicate the success of network initiatives to a broader audience, success stories of single network initiatives are also recommended. Networks do not only need the support of top management, but also support from and engagement by the company's employees.

While the external measurement part illustrates network performance on a company level, the internal measurement part shows the individual network performance and helps to monitor it. The internal measurement part consists of the newly developed individual network performance survey (INPS) and the health check for knowledge networks. Both instruments help the network leader to monitor the performance of single networks and to find areas of improvement. The health check does this with questions derived from the methodology of setting up knowledge networks for growth and checks if all recommended components are working properly. The INPS analyses the individual quality of single networks for growth and helps to identify the optimal component quality needed to fulfill the network's task.

Thus, the integrated measurement system serves to monitor and improve network performance on a company and a network level. However, returning to one of the first arguments, knowledge management activities follow middle- and long-term goals, therefore it is difficult to measure performance and influence on the company's growth goals on a short-term basis. The proposed external measurement could very well offer more value over time than directly after the network's set-up. One other limitation of the presented system consists of the individual company culture and structure that result in individual network approaches. The discussed metrics are general performance measurement methods for knowledge networks for growth and need to be adapted to a company's culture and structure as well as to the individual goal the network aims to reach. Also the individual performance measurement culture of the company needs to be taken into account. In other words, the external and the internal parts might have to be adapted or complemented by other metrics such as personal appraisal systems or team rewards.

The concept of the integrated measurement system also offers several directions for future research, particularly the development of methods to adapt the general metrics to individual company culture and structure. In addition, future studies may wish to explore the potentials of this measurement system by testing and implementing the concept derived from our research in knowledge networks for growth. The presented concept can model the understanding of the influence and value of knowledge networks in supporting important strategic goals like company growth.

In summary, this article extends our understanding of a performance measurement system for knowledge networks for growth. It extends the results of existing research in performance measurement by using the results gained from the action research approach of the competence center Knowledge Networks for Growth – as presented in this book – to create the concept of an integrated measurement system.

7 Supporting the Adaptation – Templates

Adapting the methodology for your business requires gathering data from your company and, particularly, from the specific area where you want to set up the network. These templates include guidelines for identifying the goals or tasks, and rules for the adapted network. They serve to clarify motivational aspects, success factors and barriers. The suggested order of the guidelines is aimed at fast and precise data gathering to enable the construction of the network.

Interview Guidelines

Objective of the Interview Guidelines – General Recommendations

Interviews are one of the most effective ways with which to obtain true and up to date information and to establish links to possible direct and indirect participants of the network. To gain an adequate picture of the situation, we need to meet a number of different groups whose members have varying professional backgrounds, positions and interest in the network. To overcome this problem, the interview questions should be modified for each of the involved groups.

The interview guidelines used in the steps depend on information that the knowledge network initiator does not possess. The related steps are: "Perform a Stakeholder Analysis", "Facilitate the relationships within the network", and "Choose and organize appropriate rewards and incentives".

In the following we present general recommendations for interview preparation and execution.

The Interview Process

Introduction
- Introduce yourself.
- Confirm the duration of the interview.
- Describe the background to the interview.
- Clarify the benefits of the interview for the interview partner, and review the agenda.
- Assess the communication style, attitudes, expectations and concerns of the interviewee.
- Ask initial (open) questions on, e.g., the interviewee's background in respect of knowledge or knowledge network activities.

Structured interview
- Be flexible in covering the agenda.
- Use semi structured interview guidelines to gather data for adapting the roadmap.

Conclusion
- Summarize and confirm the information.
- Collect documentation material.
- Ask about any remaining open issues and be on the alert for revealing remarks.
- Thank the interview partner and keep the possibility of another visit open.

Follow-up
- Did you manage to build a relationship with the interviewee?
- Did you obtain all the information you needed?
- What are the next steps?

Structure of the Interview Guidelines

Establish objectives
- Define minimum or optimum results.
- Set limits for the interview.

Structure contents: organize the topics logically
- According to importance and sensitivity.
- From the general to the specific.
- From the external to the internal.
- From the past to the present.

Example of the Interview Guidelines

In preparing interview guidelines to investigate the situation before the launch of the innovation network, it could be useful to run through the main steps of the methodology for the three different network levels (facilitating conditions, knowledge processes and network architecture) and to identify those that are critical for this particular network.

Interview guidelines

Welcome/procedure

1. Welcome and introduction

2. Purpose of the interview

3. Confidentiality issues

General Questions

1. Name:
2. Function:
3. Location of the interview:
4. Date and time:
5. Short biography of the interviewee (career, current position, connection to the innovation processes):

Network Specification

	Question:	Comments and direct citations:
	Network Vision	
1.	What is your view of...?	
2.	What is the current approach to...?	
3.	How could a network help you? What would you like to obtain from such a network?	
	Network Processes	
4.	What would you define as an output of the network?	
5.	What are the possible tasks of the network?	
6.	Who should be involved in this network? What are their roles and responsibilities?	
7.	What would motivate you to participate in such a network?	
8.	Should there be a Steering Committee?	
9.	What could be the network's financing sources?	
10.	How would you measure the network output?	
11.	What are the success factors for the network? What are potential barriers?	
	Network Architecture	
12.	What ICT tools should support the network?	
	Examples	
13.	What good/bad examples could you provide? Why were these so successful/unsuccessful?	

Fig. 7.1 Interview guidelines

The Business Plan

Objective of the Business Plan

"Top management will only back projects that have a well-prepared business plan."

(Looser and Schläpfer, 2001, p. xii)

> A business plan serves to obtain the support of top management and the resources required for setting up and successfully developing a network.
> The main chapter related to this template is "Facilitate Top Management and find sponsors".

Preparation of the Business Plan

How Is a Business Plan Drawn Up?

- Interview people responsible for the corresponding knowledge field.
- Reveal the gaps in knowledge and help to bridge them in an efficient and structured way.
- Quantify the costs. List the resources that will be needed, and thus reveal which resources will have to be acquired, e.g.:
  - The time team members have to spend on meetings and communication.
  - System support, such as an intranet.
  - Training.
  - Facilitation.
  - Administrative support.
- Quantify the outcomes. Plan the results of the actions and analyze how they fit in with the company's strategy.
- Prepare a short and precise description of the results of the analysis.
- Use it as a communication tool with which to approach the various partners.
- Remember that it is a dry run for the real thing. No damage is done if the business-planning phase reveals that the network is likely to fail.

Structure of the Business Plan

Title page
- Name of the network and the business area it is aimed to work in.
- Name of the initiator or leader.
- Provide an abstract on the network's relevance and need, costs and benefits.

Text
- 2-5 pages
  - The goal of the network on the local level.
  - The link of the network goal to the corporate strategy.
  - The tasks of the network (short and long term).
  - Resources required and costs expected.
  - Benefits or revenues expected to be obtained.
  - Steps completed thus far.
- Provide a clear structure with subtitles and indents.

Charts, illustrations, and tables
- A maximum of 4 illustrations as an appendix.
- Only if necessary to understand the idea.
- Explicit references in text to these.
- Simple, clear design.
- Corporate style.

Presentations to Convince Management

Objective of the Presentation to Management

The presentation of the future network to management is a first interaction with the people who have to decide if the existence of the network is feasible. The objective of this first interaction is to provide a clear and convincing picture of why the network will specially benefit the company in this time and place.

This template is used in the step "Facilitate Top Management commitment and find sponsors".

Preparation of the Presentation to Management

Ask yourself:
- Who will be receiving my message?
- What is their role?
- How will they react to my message?
- How can I convince them?
- What form of communication do they prefer?

Structure of the Presentation to Management

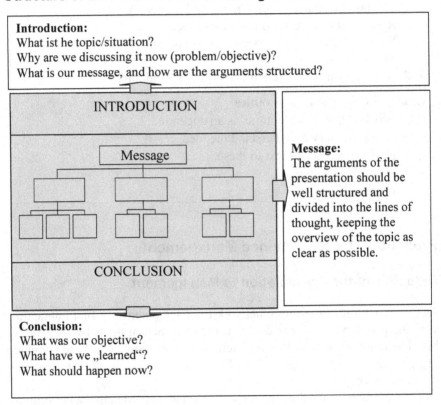

Introduction:
What ist he topic/situation?
Why are we discussing it now (problem/objective)?
What is our message, and how are the arguments structured?

INTRODUCTION

Message

Message:
The arguments of the presentation should be well structured and divided into the lines of thought, keeping the overview of the topic as clear as possible.

CONCLUSION

Conclusion:
What was our objective?
What have we „learned"?
What should happen now?

Fig. 7.2 Structure of the presentation to management

Example of the Presentation to Management

Strategy

- Gain a sustainable competitive advantage by delivering a next-generation customer experience with the establishment of a Customer Knowledge Network which puts the customer at the center of our business

Structure

- Establish a working framework and define standard proceedings, which lays the foundation for continued customer involvement in all of our activities
- The Knowledge Network presents a unified front to the customer by including members from the various organizations (based on the given task)in a common collaboration zone

Measurement

- Immediate impact on TMI, TCE and CRE measures through direct customer involvement
- The network sets priorities and de-fines the right investments to support the strategy

Culture/Behavior

- Requires support from the whole organization
- Balance risks and rewards
- Focus on "low-hanging fruits"

February 10, 2003   *Claudia Ulrich*   Page 3

Project Overview

- Objective: Develop and Imple-ment a mutual learning system that helps the customer and HP to strengthen their relationship and helps to foster the reinvention of HP's
  processes and services into a customer-focused organization

Deliverables

- Standardized procedure to obtain a consistent framework
- The framework is defined and based on Merlin methodology and TCE Proceeding
- Leverage knowledge and experi-ence to a more global pic-ture/framework
- Act on behalf of customers, bring their voice into every conversa-tion, decision and action

February 10, 2003   *Claudia Ulrich*   Page 4

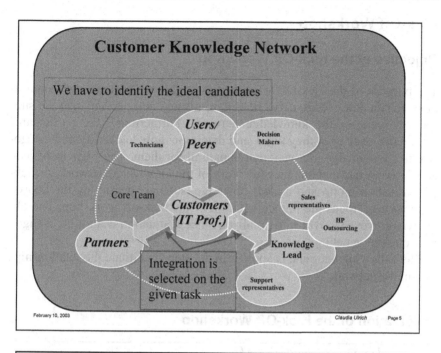

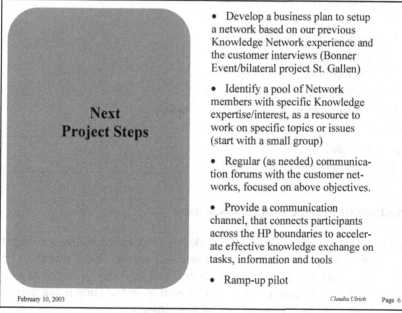

Fig. 7.3 Example presentation to management

Kick-Off Workshop

Objective of the Kick-Off Workshop

The purpose of the kick-Off workshop is to gain the participants' commitment for the knowledge network, and to discuss and particularize the subsequent work of the knowledge network. Furthermore, the participants should discover what they know and determine how to classify and categorize this knowledge in a way that is natural for them. The participants can create social ties that enhance the work of the knowledge network. A kick-off workshop motto and a clear objective, such as identifying the knowledge owners, focus the implementation of the kick-off workshop. The objective, however, ought to be realistic since a situation cannot be changed by a one-day meeting.

The following template is applied in the step "Facilitate the relationships within the network".

Preparation of the Kick-Off Workshop

Knowledge network leader's tasks:

- Preparation of the presentations.
- Preparation of the agenda.
- Preparation of the working session.
- Preparation of a list with task samples.
- Send off invitations to the kick-off workshop.

Members' tasks:
- Preparation of documents needed.

Structure of the Kick-Off Workshop

A generic structure for a kick-Off workshop is outlined below. During the kick-off workshop, the following participants are involved: members, the knowledge network leader, and managers. The first day is aimed at introducing the participants to one another as well as to the knowledge network concept. The second day ought to be a working day.

__Agenda__

Schedule	Topic	Speaker / Moderator
8.30-8.45	Introduction and welcome speech.	Sponsor
8.45-9.15	Presentation of the agenda and introduction to the expert cards working session.	Network leader
9.15-10.15	Introductions and filling in of the expert cards.	Members
10.15-10.30	Coffee break.	
10.30-11.00	Presentation on the concept of a knowledge network and of the objective of the kick-off workshop.	Network leader
11.00-12.00	Questions and answers.	All
12.00-13.00	Lunch.	
13.00-13.30	Presentation on the task or processes to be solved.	Network leader
13.30-15.00	Working session.	
15.00-17.00	Presentation, discussion of and reflection on the identified tasks and processes to be solved. Pay attention to the time, and know the content of the presentation in advance. The knowledge network leader has to identify an interesting task and processes in advance and has to discuss the topics with the mediation managers.	Members
	Discussion of the scope and responsibilities of the knowledge network. What will the scope of the knowledge network be? What are the responsibilities of the participants? What are the roles of the participants? Discussion and determination of the rules of the game for the specific network, i.e. communication rules, commitment, confidentiality, frequency of the face-to-face meetings, rules of virtual work, decision on necessary tools (databases, intranet pages etc.). The output of this discussion has to be: an agreed scope for the knowledge network, agreed roles and responsibilities.	Network leader
17.00-17.30	Wrap-up and close.	Network leader

| | Dinner and evening activity. | |
| 18.00-22.00 | This is an opportunity for the participants to get to know one another better and to socialize. | All |

Schedule	Topic	Speaker / Moderator
9.00-9.30	Introduction: Summary of previous day's results.	Network leader
9.30-10.00	Presentation on the chosen task or process to be solved in more detail.	Network leader
10.00-12.00	Working on the first short-term tasks: presentations, workshops etc.	All
	The participants divide into working groups. Each group needs an experienced moderator.	
	The network leader has to think about the composition of the working groups. This is highly important, because every participant has to participate in the network.	Members
12.00-13.00	Lunch.	
13.00-14.00	Presentation of the outcomes of the working groups.	Members
14.00-15.00	Discussion of the outcomes.	All
15.00-16.00	Wrap-up and scheduling of the next meeting.	Members
16.00-18.00	Closure.	All

Customer Knowledge Network Kick-Off Workshop Example

The example comes from the one-day customer event at Ratingen and follows the following structure:

- Part 1: Welcoming address.
- Part 2: Introduction to knowledge sharing.
- Part 3: Introduction to the knowledge network.
- Part 4: Our vision: HP's customer knowledge network, teamwork and discussion.
- Part 5: Classification of the results in the HP customer knowledge network.
- Part 6: Wrap-up.

Part 1: Welcome address

The aim of this part of the customer event is to prepare customers for the subsequent presentations, teamwork session, and the presentation of the agenda. In this part of the kick-Off workshop the previous results, i.e. personal support and commitment, have to be shown. The customer has to be shown how the event and the network are integrated in the company strategy, which serves as a basis for customer integration.

The introduction is facilitated by the company manager.

Part 2: Introduction (knowledge sharing generates reciprocating values)

The introduction should explain to the customers what the company understands under the term knowledge sharing and what the advantages of knowledge sharing are, i.e. knowledge sharing generates reciprocating values. The reciprocating knowledge sharing creates a win-win situation, and therefore it creates a competitive advantage for both.

It is presented by the knowledge network leader.

Part 3: Introduction to knowledge networks as a tool for knowledge sharing

The introduction should allow the customers to visualize knowledge network as a tool for knowledge sharing as well as explaining the potential of the knowledge network to them. For a better understanding of the principles of the knowledge network, the knowledge network initiators first have to explain the different knowledge types (i.e. explicit and implicit knowledge) as well as the different possibilities according to which these knowledge types can be stored and shared.

The concept of the knowledge network is to be illustrated with a general and self-explanatory example: BMW uses knowledge networks between engineers in the Formula 1 development unit and the engineers in the serial production that led to an improvement of the new 7th BMW model. The theoretical background of the knowledge network was explained by means of the "reference model knowledge network".

Presented by the knowledge network leader and a scholar.

Part 4: Our Vision: The HP customer knowledge network

This part should prepare the customer for the teamwork to follow. The customers are directly addressed as the possible members of the knowledge network and they are directly asked for their assistance.

Presented by the knowledge network leader and implemented by the participants.

Part 5: Classification of the results in the customer HP knowledge network - Vision
The first section summarizes the results and integrates them into the reference model. Emphasize that the results are part of the vision and that this will be communicated to the management.
Presented by the participants.
Part 6: Wrap-up
The last part highlights the customer event by, e.g., extending the vision with the day's results and creating the knowledge network with the customers.
Presented by the knowledge network leader and the manager.

Expert Cards

The expert cards serve to get to know one another and are the preconditions for the subsequent yellow pages, since they are a means to easily record personal data. The captured data are also a short-term result of the kick-off workshop. There are two ways of doing this. First, the participants fill in the expert cards at the beginning of the kick-off workshop. Second, when a participant reveals his expertise at the beginning of the first day, this is recorded by one of the other participants, which enhances his knowledge and appreciation of his counterpart.

Expert card

Name

_____

_____

Expertise and Core Competencies

A _____

B _____

C _____

D _____

My affiliation to the company: _____

_____

_____

Hobbies: _____

_____

A community I belong to: _____

_____

Why are you (still) participant of the community? _____

_____

Have you learnt anything of value in this network? (brief outline)

_____

_____

Fig. 7.4 Expert card

Outline of Communication

Objective of the Communication Outline

The objectives of the communication plan are twofold. Firstly, it serves as a means of communicating the results to the management so that they may subsequently exercise control over the work of the knowledge network. Secondly, it forms the basis for the cooperation of the knowledge network members, since they have to agree to the results and address unresolved problems of the work done in the knowledge network.

The communication outline can be designed as in the step "Justification and Communication Plan".

Structure of the Communication Outline

The following generic structure gives an outline of the issues to be considered in a communication plan.

The communication plan begins with a short but descriptive title or name for the knowledge network from which the reader ought to grasp what the topic of the knowledge network is. An indication of the time and purpose of the meeting facilitates comprehension.

The second point is a synopsis of the achieved results. None of the results should be described in more than one or two lines.

The third point addresses the business need and the business context. It describes the challenges to be solved by the knowledge network and their relevance and interrelation with the daily business.

The outcomes of the meeting and the potential outcomes of the work of the knowledge network require a qualitative description. Also describe how the results were and will be achieved. The description of the value of the achievement for the business unit or the operating department is very important. The main issue to be raised in this point is the contribution that the results make to the business unit or operating department. A qualitative, quantitative or even financial description of the outcomes is appropriate here.

The outcomes of a knowledge network are sometimes not easy for outsiders or management to grasp. You therefore need to clarify why the knowledge network is significant in terms of the outcomes to be achieved.

Knowledge gains value when it is shared (Wilke and Krück, 2001), therefore the proliferation of the results across the company is crucial. If possible, the communication plan should contain a description of the further applicability of the results, and a possible way of proliferation.

Example of a Communication Plan

M&A Knowledge Network

Synopsis of the results
- Kick-off workshop of the Nth and N^{th} of Month Year. Indication of the actual integration projects and creation of yellow pages.

Business need and business context
- Various business units carry out integration projects in the field of street lighting. The lack of communication between the people involved does not allow the utilization of the synergies that can be gained from linking their knowledge. This leads to higher costs in the realization of integration projects and in search costs.

Meeting outcomes
- The actual integration projects with the allotted persons, their responsibility, financial resources and the status of the projects have to be indicated. The assignment of people involved in the integration projects specifically provides an opportunity to reveal their field of expertise. This is achieved through a discussion and a working group session with the participants and with their experience recorded on expert cards.

Value relatedness of the outcomes for other business units
- The expert cards provide transparency regarding skills for others who are looking for relevant experts on certain topics.

Results of the outcomes and the M&A knowledge network
- Due to the geographical dispersion and work overload, the chances of formal meetings are almost non-existent. The kick-off workshop as the initial starting point of the knowledge network provides an opportunity to gather the relevant people. The structured approach of the meeting allows the actual projects to be revealed and provides transparency regarding the field of expertise of the people involved.

The integration and communication of the knowledge network's outcomes
- The transparency of the field of expertise, i.e. expert cards, can be accessed by others employees. The experiences with the structure of the kick-off workshop can be used to set up other knowledge networks.

Internal Performance Measurement System

Objective of the Internal Performance Measurement System

The objective of the internal performance measurement system is to frequently provide an adequate picture of the internal network performance. As network performance is evaluated by both the network leader and its members, this measurement system ensures that a network is highly valued.

This internal measurement system opens the "black box" of the network processes and allows fast response to emerging problems.

The conventional external measurements of network performance, which primarily examine the network interactions with the environment (opportunities and threats), could be beneficially enriched with internal network measurements that examine the internal processes of the network (strengths and weaknesses).

The following template is based on step "Internal Performance Measurement".

Structure of the Internal Performance Measurement System

The internal performance measurement system (IPMS) ensures the development of an individual measurement system for each network through its flexible structure that allows selection and emphasizing of areas specific to this network.

The two major components of the IPMS are the network performance survey (INPS) and the health check. These two measures differ in their purposes: while the health check is aimed at regular monitoring of the network performance and is conducted by the network leader, the INPS measures the network outcomes and efficiency and, since it covers all network members and encourages substantial efforts, has to be performed less frequently.

Table 7.1 Example of the internal performance measurement system

Internal Performance Measurement System		
	Health Check	**Individual Network Performance Survey (INPS)**
people involved	network leader	all network members
frequency of measuring	often	seldom
Purpose of measuring	monitoring of the performance	efficiency indication outcome measure

The health check is comprised of a questionnaire that has to be answered by the network leader on a regular basis. The suggested areas of the network to be analyzed are given below.

- Network alignment with corporate vision and growth strategy/ communication.
- Facilitate top-management commitment/ knowledge board.
- Identify your goals, task and activities.
- Facilitate relationships within the network.
- Facilitate relationships with the outside world.
- Establish measurements.

The INPS is comprised of the questionnaire and the table that are both aimed at the detailing of certain aspects of the network performance.

The questionnaire could start with open questions on the goal and the tasks of the network, followed by closed questions on the quality and importance of the different components and could close with open questions on the success and failure of the network.

The figure below is aimed at providing a detailed and visually easy to understand representation of the of the network members' opinions on the network performance.

Characteristics Components	(1) Quality of the component in your network	(2) Importance of your task fulfilment	Difference $(1)-(2)$
Strong management support	(number)	(number)	
Strong link to the corporate knowledge vision and strategy	(number)	(number)	
Right people in the network	(number)	(number)	
Rewards and Incentives are in place for the work of the members	(number)	(number)	
...			

Fig. 7.5 Network questionnaire

Project Plan

Objective of the Project Plan

The project plan is aimed at providing a detailed description of the steps required for building a network. It is based on the business plan written for the management, and is addressed at those who build the network. The main objective of the project plan is to make the building of the network visible and to optimally plan the time required for it.

Preparation of the Project Plan – General Recommendations

Detailed analysis of the project
- Start with the major network tasks being identified.
- Prioritize tasks.
- Identify which actions are critical to ensure the realization of these tasks.
- Plan the order of the steps required for the launch of the network.
- Check which steps could be realized simultaneously.
- Make use of the experts' advice.
- Be flexible.
- And apply the 80/20 formula of effective time use.

The related step is chapter "Methodology at a Glance: The Project Plan".

8 References

Alba, R. D. (1982). Taking Stock of Network Analysis: A Decade's Results. Research in the sociology of organizations. Bachatach, S. B. Greenwich: 39-74.

Allen, T. J. (1977). Managing the Flow of Technology. Technology Transfer and the Dessemission of Technological Information within R&D Organization. MIT Press. Cambridge, London.

Arveson, P. (1999). The Balanced Scorecard and Knowledge Management, http://www.balancedscorecard.org/bscand/bsckm.html.

Back, A., von Krogh, G., Seufert, A. & Enkel, E. (Eds.) (2005). Putting Knowledge Networks into Action. Methodology, Development, Maintenance. Springer Verlag. Berlin, Heidelberg, New York.

Back, A.; von Krogh, G.; Seufert, A. & Enkel, E. (Eds.) (2006). Getting Real about Knowledge Networks: Unlocking Corporate Knowledge Assets, Palgrave MacMillan. Hampshire, UK.

Badaracco, J. L. (1991). The knowledge link: How firms compete through strategic alliances. Harvard Business School Press. Boston (MA).

Baden-Fuller, C. (1992). Rejuvenating the mature business: The competitive challenge. Routledge and Kegan. London.

Birkinshaw, J., Bresman, H. & Hakanson, L. (2000). Managing the post - acquisition integration process: how the human integration and task integration processes interact to foster value creation. Journal of Management Studies. 37 (3): 395-425.

Brown, J. S. (2002). Research that reinvents the corporation. Harvard Business Review. 80 (8): 117-127.

Büchel, B. and Raub, S. (2002). Building Knowledge-creating Value Networks. European Management Journal. 20 (6): 587-596.

Buono, A. F. and Bowditch, J. L. (1989). The human side of mergers and acquisitions: Managing collisions between people and organizations. Jossey Bass. San Francisco.

Christ, O. (2001). Content Management Architektur: Strategien, Prozessmodelle, Softwarelösungen, Projektszenarien. Institut für Wirtschaftsinformatik, Universität St. Gallen. St. Gallen.

Christensen, C. M. (1997). The Innovator's Dilemma: When New Technologies Cause Great Firms to Fail. Harvard Business School Press. Boston (MA).

Cohen, L., Manion, L. & Morrison, K. (2000). Research methods in education. RoutledgeFalmer. London.

Cohen, W. M. and Levinthal, D. (1990). Absorptive Capacity: A New Perspective on Learning and Innovation. Administrative Science Quarterly. 35 (1): 128-152.

Connolly, S. and Klein, L. (2002). The impact of a merger on Novell's KM efforts: How KM survived and even set the tone for a new organization. Knowledge Management Review. 5 (4): 21-24.

Cross, R., Borgatti, S. & Parker, A. (2002). Using social network analysis to support strategic collaboration. California Management Review. 44 (2): 25-46.

Davenport, T. H., Harris, J. G. & Kohli, A. K. (2001). How do they know their customers so well. Sloan Management Review. 63.

Davenport, T. H. and Prusak, L. (1998). Working Knowledge: How Organizations Manage what They Know. Harvard Business School Press. Boston (MA).

Drucker, P. (1991). The Discipline of Innovation. In: Managing Innovation. Henry, J. and Walkner, D. Sage. London: 9-17.

Drucker, P. (2002). The Discipline of Innovation. Harvard Business Review. 80 (8): 95-101.

Empson, L. (2001). Fear of exploitation and fear of contamination: Impedients to knowledge transfer in mergers between professional service firms. Human Relations. 54 (7): 839-862.

Enkel, E. (2005). Management von Wissen durch Wissensnetzwerke. Erfolgsfaktoren und Beispiele. Deutscher Universitäts-Verlag Gabler. Wiesbaden.

Flamholtz, E. G. (1989). Human Resource Accounting. McGraw-Hill. New York.

Frey, B. S. and Osterloh, M. (2000). Motivation, Knowledge Transfer, and Organizational Forms. Organization Science. 11 (5): 538-550.

Garcia-Murillo, M. and Annabi, H. (2002). Customer knowledge management. Journal of the Operational Research Society. 53 (8): 875-884.

Gassmann, O. and Enkel, E. (2005): Gestaltung globaler F&E-Netzwerke. Von Struktur und Prozess zu Person und Wissen. Controlling. 8/9: 460-466.

Gertz, D. L. and Baptista, J. P. A. (1995). Grow to be Great: Breaking the Downsizing Cycle. Free Press. New York (NY).

Gibbert, M., Leibold, M. & Probst, G. J. B. (2002). Five styles of Customer Knowledge Management, and how smart companies use them to create value. European Management Journal. 20 (5): 459-469.

Giddens, A. (1984). The Constitution of Society - Outline of the Theory of Structure. University of California Press. Berkeley.

Gongla, P. and Rizzuto, C. R. (2001). Evolving communities of practice: IBM Global Service experience. IBM Systems Journal. 40 (4): 842-863.

Govindarajan, V. and Gupta, A. K. (2001). Building an Effective Global Business Team. Sloan Management Review. 42 (4): 63-71.

Hackman, J. R. (1990). Groups that work (and those that don't) creating conditions for effective teamwork. Jossey-Bass. San Francisco (CA)

Haspelagh, P. C. and Jemison, D. B. (1991). Managing Acquisitions: Creating Value through Corporate Renewal. The Free Press. New York (NY).

Henderson, R. and Clark, K. B. (1990). Architectural innovation: The reconfiguration of consisting product technologies and the failure of established firms. Administrative Science Quarterly. 35: 9-30.

Honegger, J. (2002). Systematisches Komplexitätsmanagement - Die Methode "Vernetztes Denken und Handeln". Netmap. Teufen: 1-39.

Jansen, S. A. (2002). Pre- und Post Merger-Integration in Cross Border Transactions: Trends, Tools, Theses, and Empirical Tests of Old and New Economy Deals. IESE: 1-29.

Jarvenpaa, S. L. and Leidner, D. E. (1999). Communication and Trust in Global Virtual Teams. Organization Science. 10 (6): 791-815.

Kano, N. (1984). Attractive Quality and Must-be Quality. Hinshitsu: The Journal of the Japanese Society for Quality Control. 14 (2): 39-48.

Kanter, R. M. (1988). When a Thousand Flowers Bloom: Structural, Collective, and Social Conditions for Innovation in Organizations. Research in Organizational Behaviour. 10: 169.

Kaplan, R. S. and Norton, D. P. (1992). The Balanced Scorecard - Measures that Drive Perfomance. Harvard Business Review. 70 (1): 71-79.

Katz, R. and Tushman, M. (1979). Communication patterns, project performance, and task characteristics: An empirical evaluation and integration in an R&D setting. Management Science. 28 (2): 135-155.

Kay, I. T. and Shelton, M. (2000). The people problem in mergers. McKinsey Quarterly. 4: 26-27.

Kenney, M. (2001). The Temporal Dynamics of Knowledge Creation in the Information Society. In: Nonaka, I. and Nishiguchi, T. (2001) Knowledge Emergence: Social, Technical, and Evolutionary Dimensions of Knowledge Creation. Oxford University Press. Oxford et al.: 93-110.

Kim, W. C. and Mauborgne, R. (1997). Value innovation: The strategic logic of high growth. Harvard Business Review. 75 (1): 102-112.

Kodama, F. (1995). Emerging patterns of innovation: Sources of Japans's technological edge. Harvard Business School Press. Boston (MA).

Kodama, M. (2002). Strategic Partnerships With Innovative Customers: A Japanese Case Study. Information Systems Management. Spring: 31-52.

Kvale, S. (1996). Interviews: An introduction to qualitative research interviewing. Sage Publications. Thousand Oaks (CA).

Leonard-Barton, D. (1995). Wellsprings of knowledge: Building and sustaining the source of innovation. Harvard Business School Press. Boston (MA).

Levinthal, D. and March, J. G. (1993). The myopia of learning. Strategic Management Journal. 14 (8: Special Issue: Organizations, Decision Making and Strategy): 95-112.

Lincoln, J. R. (1982). Intra- (and Inter-) organizational networks. Research in the sociology of organizations. Bacharach, S. B. Greenwich: 255-294.

Looser, U. and Schläpfer, B. (2001). The New Venture Adventure: Succeed with Professional Business Planning. Texere. New York (NY).

Mergerstat (2000). Mergerstat.com, March 2003.

Mitchell, J. C. (1969). The Concept and Use of Social Networks. Social networks in urban situations. Mitchell, J. C. Manchester University Press. Manchester: 1-12.

Morosini, P., Shane, S. & Singh, H. (1998). National Culture Distance and Cross-Border Acquisition Performance. Journal of International Business Studies. 29 (1): 137-158.

Moser, T. and Moukanas, H. (2002). Setting the agenda. Mercer Management Journal. (13): 1-13.

Nahapiet, J. and Ghoshal, S. (1998). Social capital, intellectual capital, and the organizational advantage. Academy of Management Review. 23 (2): 242-261.

Nishiguchi, T. and Beaudet, A. (1998). The Toyota Group and the Aisin Fire. Sloan Managemenet Review. 40 (1): 49-59.

Nonaka, I. and Takeuchi, H. (1995). The Knowledge Creating Company: How Japanese Companies Create the Dynamics of Innovation. Oxford University Press. New York (NY).

Nooteboom, B. (1999). The dynamic efficiency of networks. Interfirm Networks. Grandori A. Routledge. London: 91-119.

North, K. (1999). Wissensorientierte Unternehmensführung Wertschöpfung durch Wissen. Gabler. Wiesbaden.

North, K. and Blanco, A. (2003). Wissen fusionieren: Wie Wissensintegration den Erfolg von Mergers and Acquisitions unterstützt. New Management. 72 (4): 36-45.

Norton, D. (2000). Strategic Enterprise Management - Strategien erfolgreich umsetzen: Die Balanced Scorecard. SAP AG, 2002.

Parker, A., Cross, R. & Walsh, D. (2001). Improving Collaboration with Social Network Analysis. Knowledge Management Review. 4 (2): 24-28.

Picot, A., Reichwald, R. & Wigand, R. (2001). Die grenzenlose Unternehmung. Gabler. Wiesbaden.

Pierer, H. v. (2000). Knowledge as Competitive Advantage. In: Davenport, T. H. and Probst, G.: Knowledge Management Case Book: Siemens Best Practices. München: 5-6.

Polanyi, M. (1966). The Tacit Dimension. Routledge & Kegan Paul. New York.

Powell, W. W. (1990). Neither Market Nor Hierarchy - Network Forms of Organization. Research in Organizational Behavior. 12: 295-336.

Probst, G. and Gomez, P. (1991). Vernetztes Denken. Ganzheitliches Führen in der Praxis. Gabler. Wiesbaden.

Probst, G. and Knaese, B. (1999). Risiko von Wissensverlusten als Folge von Mergers & Acquisitions. Bilanz Manager. 3 (4): 11-15.

Quinn, B. (1992). Intelligent Enterprise - A Knowledge and Service Based Paradigm for Industry. The Free Press. New York (NY).

Raimann, J. (2002). Unterstützung von Wissensnetzwerken mit I-Net-basierten Informations- und Kommunikationstechnologien Konzepte, Dienstemodell, Vorgehen. Difo-Druck. Bamberg.

Raimann, J., Köhne, M., Seufert, A., von Krogh, G. & Back, A. (2000). Performance Measurement of Communities of Practice. Working Paper BE HSG / IWI3 Nr. 17, Knowledge Source University of St.Gallen. St.Gallen.

Senge, P. (1990). The Fifth Discipline. Doubleday. New York (NY).

Seufert, A., Back, A. & von Krogh, G. (1999). Towards Knowledge Networking. Journal of Knowledge Management. 3 (3): 180-190.

Stajkovic, A. D. and Luthans, F. (2001). Differential effects of incentive motivators on work performance. Academy of Management Journal. 44 (3): 580-591.

Strassmann, P. A. (1996). The Value of Computer, Information and Knowledge. strassmann.com.

Sviokla, J. J. and Shapiro, B. P. (1993). Keeping customers. Harvard Business School Press. Boston (MA).

Teece, D. J. (1986). Profiting from technological innovation: Implications for integration, collaboration, licensing and public policy. Research Policy. 15 (6): 285-305.

Tichy, N., Tushman, M. & Fombrun, C. (1979). Social Networks Analysis for Organizations. Academy of Management Journal. 4: 507-519.

Tschirky, H. and Koruna, S. (Eds.) (1998). Technologie-Management. Verlag Industrielle Organisation. Zürich.

Tuckman, B. W. (1965). Developmental Sequence in Small Groups. Psychological Bulletin. 63 (6): 384-199.

Vassiliadis, S., Buzzi, G. & Seufert, A. (1999). @vantage: Nutzenpotentiale für Wissensmanagement. KnowledgeSource Working Paper No. 6 University of St. Gallen. St.Gallen.

Vassiliadis, S., Köhne, M., Seufert, A., Back, A. & von Krogh, G. (2000). Strategic Deployment of Networks for Knowledge Management. In: Working Paper Research Center KnowledgeSource. St. Gallen, University of St. Gallen, BE HSG/ IWI 3 Nr. 13/IfB Nr. 41.

von Hippel, E. (1988). The Source of Innovation. Oxford University Press. New York (NY).

von Hippel, E. (1994). "Sticky Information" and the Locus of Problem Solving: Implications for Innovation. Management Science. 40.

von Krogh, G., Ichijo, K. & Nonaka, I. (2000). Enabling Knowledge Creation: How to Unlock the Mystery of Tacit Knowledge and Release the Power of Innovation. Oxford University Press. New York (NY).

von Krogh, G., Nonaka, I. & Aben, M. (2001a). Alternatives Knowledge Strategies. Working Paper.

von Krogh, G., Nonaka, I. & Aben, M. (2001b). Making the Most of Your Company's Knowledge: A Strategic Framework. Long Range Planning. 34 (4): 421-439.

von Krogh, G. and Venzin, M. (1995). Anhaltende Wettbewerbsvorteile durch Wissensmanagement. Die Unternehmung. 95 (6): 417-435.

Wasserman, S. and Faust, K. (1994). Social network analysis : methods and applications. Cambridge University Press. New York (NY).

Wenger, E. (1998). Communities of Practices. Cambridge University Press. New York (NY).

Wenger, E. (2001). Supporting communities of practice: A survey of community-oriented technologies.

Wenger, E. (2002). Cultivating Communities of Practice: A Guide to Managing Knowledge. Harvard Business School Press. Boston (MA)

Wenger, E., McDermott, R. A. and Snyder, W. (2002). Cultivating Communities of Practice: A Guide to Managing Knowledge. Harvard Business School Press. Boston (MA).

Wilke, H. and Krück, C. (2001). Systemisches Wissensmanagement. Lucius & Lucius. Stuttgart.

Wood, R. C. and Hamel, G. (2002). The World Bank's Innovation Market. Harvard Business Review. 80 (11): 104-111.

Wysocki, B. (1997). Why an acquisition? Often, it's the people. Wall Street Journal. 10 (6).

9 List of Figures

10 List of Tables

11 Index

12 Authors

Prof. Dr. Andrea Back
is director of the Institute of Information Management at the University of St. Gallen. Her research focuses on knowledge and learning management. She founded the KnowledgeSource in 1998 and supervised the two competence centres Knowledge Networks and Knowledge Networks for Business Growth.

Dr. Ellen Enkel
has been leading the competence centre Open Innovation at the Institute of Technology Management at the University of St. Gallen since 2003. She is vice head of the chair of Innovation Management and lecturer for knowledge and innovation management. She led the competence centre Knowledge Networks for Business Growth from 2000 till 2003.

Dr. Grzegorz Gurgul
was research assistant and PhD student for the competence centre Knowledge Networks for Business Growth from 2001-2003. His doctoral thesis focused on potentials of external knowledge integration into internal networks and was finished in 2006.

Carl-Heinrich Kruse
was leading the human resources department, responsible for personnel development at RWE NET since 2004. He is now leading partner of a consultancy company for human resource management. His work focuses on the human aspects of knowledge management. He was representative for RWE Net in the competence centre Knowledge Networks for Business Growth from 2001 till 2003.

Kordula Schulte
is working in the human resources department Východoslovenská energetika (VE) within the RWE group. Her work focuses on the human aspects of knowledge management. She was representative for RWE Net in

the competence centre Knowledge Networks for Business Growth from 2001 till 2003.

Dr. Anita Pos

has been a senior member of the Unilever knowledge management group for many years and in this role she has been involved in diverse projects on knowledge strategy, communities of practice and innovation. She has joined CIBITs knowledge- and innovation management group in 2005.

Dr. Maria Rumyantseva

was research assistant and PhD student for the competence centre Knowledge Networks for Business Growth from 2001-2003. Her doctoral thesis focused on externalization of research and deveopment and was finished in 2006.

Claudia Ulrich

is working in the „Information Technology Resource Center" (ITRC) at Hewlett-Packard Germany. Her work focuses on the management of customer knowledge. She was representative for Hewlett-Packard Germany in the competence centres Knowledge Networks and Knowledge Networks for Business Growth from 1999 till 2003.

Prof. Georg von Krogh

holds the chair of Strategic Management and Innovation at the Department of Management, Technology, and Economics at the ETH Zurich. His research focuses on competitive strategy and innovation. Prof. von Krogh founded the KnowledgeSource in 1998 and supervised the two competence centres Knowledge Networks and Knowledge Networks for Business Growth.